The Inevitable!

"Your business EXIT is inevitable. The big question is; will you be

EXITING at a PROFIT or LOSS?"

If you plan to exit at a LOSS, please close this workbook and save yourself some time. If you plan to exit at a PROFIT, read on. This workbook is for you.

The material is for informational and educational purposes only. This material is designed to provide general information regarding the subject matter covered. It is not intended to serve as legal, tax or other financial advice Related to an individual situation. Because each individual's legal, tax and financial situation is different, specific advice should be tailored to the particular circumstances.

For this reason, you are advised to consult with your own attorney, accountant, or tax preparer regarding your specific situation.

New Life Clarity Publishing

205 West 300 South, Brigham City, Utah 84302

Http://newlifeclarity.com/

Printed in the United States of America
ISBN- 978-1-7361193-5-8
Copyright@2020 Jeffrey Levine

Consistent Profitable Growth Map
WORKBOOK

by
Jeffrey Levine

Contents

The Inevitable Question

The inevitable question is; **how will you EXIT your business?** Many business owners are busy running their businesses, but they have not invested enough time to answer the inevitable question.

The reality is that as a business owner, you will EXIT your business at some point. Here are some reasons that will cause you to EXIT:

1. Poor Health

2. Lack of Passion

3. Tiredness

There can be other reasons that could force an exit such as death, disagreement with a partner etc. but, in this workbook, we will focus on the 3 reasons above. Let us look at each of them;

1. **Poor Health** – Health is one of the most important aspects of our lives.

   Unfortunately, many business owners do not take care of their health. They log in 50, 60, 70 and some even 80+ hours a week working while their health is deteriorating. Eventually, their health deteriorates to a point where they are forced to exit the business or die prematurely.

   If you are a business owner who is currently logging in long hours each week at the expense of your health, you will soon be forced to exit your business or die. *If your health forces you to exit your business, will you be exiting at a profit or loss?*

   If your answer was exiting at a loss or you are not even sure, in this workbook, we will show you how to prepare your business for a profitable exit.

2. **Lack of passion** – Let us face it. There are many business owners who were once passionate about their business but over the years, they have lost passion gradually and many of them are forced to exit or continue to run a business that is not fulfilling them.

   If you are a business owner who has lost passion, you will soon be forced to exit or continue to run an unfulfilled business. *If lack of passion forces you to exit your business, will you be exiting at a profit or loss?*

   If your answer was exiting at a loss or you are not even sure, in this workbook, we will show you how to prepare your business for a profitable exit.

3. **Tiredness** – Energy is one of the most important assets of running a business. If a business owner does not have energy, productivity will be very low. That is where I was when I was 47 years. I was working 7 days a week for a long time until I became so tired.

I knew the way I was running my business was not sustainable. At the same time, I knew that my business was not ready for a profitable exit, so I made a firm decision to restructure my business to exit at age of 57. Essentially, I gave myself 10 years to restructure, grow profitably and exit profitably.

*I successfully had a profitable **7-figure exit** at the age of 54 and I invested 3 more years helping the new owners with the transition and by age 57, I was completely out. My dream came true.*

If your dream is to have a profitable exit, you are holding the right workbook in your hands. In this workbook, I will show you step by step how to plan, grow and exit your business profitably with a **Consistent Profitable Growth Map** whether you are forced to exit your business due to the reasons above or you plan and exit willingly so you can focus on other things such as travel, community work or even missionary work without worrying about money.

What Is A Consistent Profitable Growth Map?

A Consistent Profitable Growth Map is a guide for business owners who desire to grow and exit profitably. The PROCESS of developing this map has 5 major steps:

1. STEP 1 – DESTINATION

2. STEP 2 – DEPARTURE

3. STEP 3 – MAP

4. STEP 4 – GROWTH ROUTINES

5. STEP 5 – ACCOUNTABILITY

On the following pages, we will look at each of these steps detailly, so you can follow along.

By the time you finish this workbook, your business will have the following:

- A clear 5 - 10 years consistent profitable growth map.

- A clear profitable growth map for one year with clear profit targets for each quarter.

- A clear profitable growth map for each quarter with a clear profit target for each week.

- A profitable growth daily routine

- A profitable growth weekly routine

- A profitable growth monthly routine

- A profitable growth quarterly routine

- A profitable growth yearly routine

You will also learn how to track your results daily, weekly, monthly, quarterly and yearly so your business can always stay on track as you navigate into a profitable future.

Let us begin with step 1.

STEP 1

DESTINATION

The most important part of every journey is the destination. Without a clear destination, it is impossible to generate a consistent growth map. To clearly define your business destination, it is important you answer some questions:

5 - 10 years from this year, how much will you like to sell your business assuming you will exit the business in 5 - 10 years?

To help you determine an accurate destination, let's talk about a standard business valuation equation. In this workbook we will be using (4 x profit) as the standard valuation equation even though valuation multiples vary from industry to industry with some industries such as Gasoline Stations (3.70) have a valuation multiple of less than 4 and other industries such as Computer Related Services (8.19) have a valuation multiple more than 4.

With this standard valuation equation, let us look at some potential exit prices and their corresponding profit targets:

Target Exit Sale Price	Target Profit
$1,000,000	$250,000
$2,000,000	$500,000
$3,000,000	$750,000
$5,000,000	$1,250,000
$9,000,000	$2,250,000

As you can see from the table above, if you desire to sell your business at exit for $1,000,000, your business should be generating at least $250,000 in profit 5 - 10 years from this year since the standard valuation equation we are using is 4 x profit. $250,000 x 4 = $1,000,000.

Whether you plan to exit at $1,000,000 or $9,000,000, the choice is yours. How do you determine the right exit amount to target? That is a good question. It depends on the lifestyle you want after you exit.

Let us take the following steps to estimate a target exit amount for your business. We will be using John's example to facilitate this exercise:

John 's Step 1: John's Lifestyle

Let us use John's example who is planning to exit his business in 5 - 10 years:

Where will John's primary home be located?

John's primary home will be located in Southlake, Texas

How many cars will John have?

John plans to have 2 cars (One for him and one for his wife)

Will John be travelling?

Yes. John plans to travel a lot since he has been working a lot with little time to travel

How much will John be giving to charity?

John plans to give about 10% of his income to charity.

Will John be supporting members of his family such as kids or grand kids?

Yes. John plans to support members of his family. He has some kids and grandkids.

Now that we have defined a post exit lifestyle with John's example, let us define your lifestyle after you exit your business.

Your Step 1: Define Your Lifestyle.

The following questions should help you define your post exit lifestyle so we can determine an appropriate business exit target amount.

Where will your primary home be located?

How many cars do you plan to have?

Will you be travelling?

_____

How much will you be giving to charity?

_____

How much will you need to support members of your family such as kids or grand kids?

_____

John's Step 2: John's Estimated Lifestyle Cost

To determine John's lifestyle cost, let us start at the level of the month:

Lifestyle	Estimated Monthly Cost (LC)
Housing	$3,000
Cars	$1,000
Travel	$1,000
Charity	$1,000
Family	$2,000
TOTAL	$8,000

Your Step 2: Determine Your Estimated Lifestyle Cost

Enter your estimated monthly cost based on the lifestyle you have described above:

Lifestyle	Estimated Monthly Cost
Housing	$
Cars	$
Travel	$
Charity	$
Family	$
TOTAL	$

John's Step 3: Add 40% To John's Estimated Lifestyle Cost

Let us add 40% to John's estimated lifestyle cost to determine his Gross Estimated Monthly Lifestyle Cost. This 40% addition will take care of anything he might have underestimated.

Lifestyle	Lifestyle Cost	40%	Gross Lifestyle Cost
Housing	$3,500	$1,400	$4,900
Cars	$1,000	$400	$1,400
Travel	$1,000	$400	$1,400
Charity	$1,000	$400	$1,400
Family	$2,000	$800	$2,800
TOTAL	**$8,500**	**$3,400**	**$11,900**

Your Step 3: Add 40% To Your Estimated Lifestyle Cost

Add 40% to your estimated lifestyle cost to determine your Gross Estimated Monthly Lifestyle Cost. This 40% addition will take care of anything you might have underestimated.

Lifestyle	Lifestyle Cost	40%	Gross Lifestyle Cost
Housing	$	$	$
Cars	$	$	$
Travel	$	$	$
Charity	$	$	$
Family	$	$	$
TOTAL	**$**	**$**	**$**

John's Step 4: Add 60% To John's Gross Estimated Lifestyle Cost

Let us add 60% to John's gross estimated lifestyle cost to determine his Taxable Gross Estimated Monthly Lifestyle Cost (TGLC). This 60% addition will take care of any applicable taxes.

Lifestyle	Gross Lifestyle Cost	60%	Total Gross Lifestyle Cost
Housing	$4,900	$2,940	$7,840
Cars	$1,400	$840	$2,240
Travel	$1,400	$840	$2,240
Charity	$1,400	$840	$2,240
Family	$2,800	$1,680	$4,480
TOTAL	**$11,900**	**$7,140**	**$19,040**

Now that we have the taxable gross living cost for the month, let us multiply it by 12 to determine the yearly amount. $19,040 x 12 = $228,480

For John to live comfortably after exiting his business, he needs a yearly passive cash flow of $228,480.

Your Step 4: Add 60% To Your Gross Estimated Lifestyle Cost

Add 60% to your gross estimated lifestyle cost (GLC) to determine your Taxable Gross Estimated Monthly Lifestyle Cost (TGLC). This 60% addition will take care of any applicable taxes.

Lifestyle	GLC	60%	TGLC
Housing	$	$	$
Cars	$	$	$
Travel	$	$	$
Charity	$	$	$
Family	$	$	$
TOTAL	$	$	$

What is your taxable gross living cost for each month? Multiply it by 12 to determine the yearly amount
$_____ x 12 = $_____

For you to live comfortably after exiting your business, you need a yearly passive cash flow of
$_____.

John's Step 5: Determine An Estimated Exit Amount And Profit Target

The goal of this step is to determine how much John needs to sell or exit his business in order to generate **$228,480** in passive cash flow as established in step 4 above. To calculate John's estimated exit amount, let us divide $228,480 by 5%. Why 5%? 5% is the minimum expected yield.

John's Estimated Exit Amount: $228,480 ÷ 5% = $4,569,600

Now let us determine the profit amount John's business needs to be generating at the time of exit. Recall that the typical business valuation equation for most industries is 4 times of the profit.

Therefore, to determine the profit amount, we simply divide the estimated exit amount ($4,569,600) by 4.

Business estimated exit profit target: $4,569,600 ÷ 4 = **$1,142,400**

In the next 5 years, John has to consistently grow the business to generate a profit of at least $1,142,400 by the time of exit. This is John's business destination.

Your Step 5: Determine Your Estimated Exit Amount And Profit Target

To determine your estimated exit amount and profit target, please answer the following questions:

- What is your estimated yearly passive cash flow amount?

- $_____

- Your Estimated Exit Amount: $_____ ÷ 5% = $_____

- Let us determine your estimated business exit profit by dividing your estimated exit amount by 4.

- Business estimated exit profit target: $_____ ÷ 4 = $_____

Your business exit estimated profit target is your **destination**.

Let us now proceed to determine your **departure**.

STEP 2
DEPARTURE

To determine your departure, we need to look at your businesses' current income statement. Before we ask you some questions about your current income statement, let us look at John's business income statement. John's business is called Small Business Growth LLC

Here is Small Business Growth, LLC 's current simplified Income Statement:

Small Business Growth, LLC
Income Statement
Year Ended December 31, 2018

Income	$350,000
Total Operating Expenses	$253,500
Profit Before Taxes	$96,500
Income Tax Expense	$9,000
Profit	$87,500

Based on the above calculations, Small Business Growth, LLC has a profit margin of **25%** (87,500 ÷ 350,000) and his tax expense percentage is **10.29%** ($9,000/87,500)

Here are some questions for you:

- What is the name of your business? _____

- How does your current simplified Income Statement look like? Use the simple template below to enter your business's current numbers:

Income Statement

Year Ended December _____

Income	
Total Operating Expenses	
Profit Before Taxes	
Income Tax Expense	
Profit	

- What is your current profit margin? (Profit ÷ Income) = _____

- What is your current tax expense percentage? (Tax Expense ÷ Profit) = _____

For your business to arrive at the desired exit destination faster, you have 3 primary goals:

1. Increase your business income consistently

2. Decrease your total operating expenses consistently

3. Decrease your income tax expense consistently

When you achieve these 3 primary goals, your profit will automatically increase consistently.

A consistent profitable growth map will enable us to achieve the three primary goals above. Let us process to design a consistent profitable growth map.

STEP 3
MAP

The purpose of a map is to guide your business from current profit – departure to exit target profit – destination.

Using Small Business Growth LLC as our example, let us design a consistent profitable growth map.

The 1st 5 Year Period:

	Departure	Year 1	Year 2	Year 3	Year 4	Year 5
	Previous Year	20%	21%	22%	23%	24%
		Growth ↑	Growth ↑	Growth ↑	Growth ↑	Growth ↑
1. Income	$350,000	$420,000	$508,200	$620,004	$762,605	$953,256
2. Profit Margin	25%	26%	27%	28%	29%	30%
3. Profit	$87,500	$109,200	$137,214	$173,601	$221,155	$285,977
Valuation	**$350,000**	**$436,800**	**$548,856**	**$694,404**	**$884,622**	**$1,143,907**

The 2nd 5 Year Period:

	Departure	Year 6	Year 7	Year 8	Year 9	Year 10
	Previous Year	27%	27%	29%	31%	33%
		Growth ↑	Growth ↑	Growth ↑	Growth ↑	Growth ↑
1. Income	$953,256	$1,210,635	$1,537,507	$1,983,384	$2,598,233	$3,455,650
2. Profit Margin	30%	31%	32%	33%	34%	35%
3. Profit	$285,977	$375,297	$492,002	$654,517	$883,399	$1,209,477
Valuation	**$1,143,907**	**$1,501,188**	**$1,968,009**	**$2,618,067**	**$3,533,597**	**$4,837,910**

As we can see from the above templates, Small Business Growth LLC started with a profit of $87,500 and the business grew for 10 years to $1,209,477. This number exceeds the exit target number of $1,142,400. John's business on track for him to exit profitably by year 10.

Now it is your turn. Use the templates below to project your numbers taking the following steps:

- **Step 1:** From your previous year's Income Statement, enter your income number, profit margin percentage (profit ÷ income), profit number and valuation number. The valuation number is simply the profit number multiplied by 4 as established above.

- **Step 2:** Project your income growth rates from year 1 through year 10.

- **Step 3:** Project your profit margin rates from year 1 through year 10.

- **Step 4:** Calculate the rest of the numbers using John's Home Cleaning business example above.

- **Step 5:** Ensure that your year 10 profit number is equal or exceeds your exit target profit number. If your projected profit number in year 10 is below your exit target profit number, review your numbers until your year 10 profit number is equal or exceeds your exit target profit number.

The 1ˢᵗ 5 Year Period:

	Departure	Year 1	Year 2	Year 3	Year 4	Year 5
	Previous Year					
		Growth ↑	Growth ↑	Growth ↑	Growth ↑	Growth ↑
1. Income						
2. Profit Margin						
3. Profit						
Valuation						

The 2ⁿᵈ 5 Year Period:

	Departure	Year 6	Year 7	Year 8	Year 9	Year 10
	Previous Year					
		Growth ↑	Growth ↑	Growth ↑	Growth ↑	Growth ↑
1. Income						
2.Profit Margin						
3. Profit						
Valuation						

As stated in step 2, for your business to arrive at the desired exit destination faster, you have 3 primary goals:

1. Increase your business income consistently

2. Decrease your total operating expenses consistently

3. Decrease your income tax expense consistently

When you achieve these 3 primary goals, your profit will automatically increase consistently.

From the 3 goals above, the most IMPORTANT goal is to increase your business income consistently because without income, you cannot pay for your expenses which will result to an unprofitable exit. Unfortunately, according to the bureau of labor statistics, more than 60% of businesses choose this exit after 10 – 15 years in business.

Since we have established that increasing your business income consistently is your most important goal, let us proceed to establish some profitable growth habits for your business starting with Small Business Growth LLC example.

Based on our projections in step 3, Small Business Growth LLC had the following projections for the 1ˢᵗ 5 years:

The 1ˢᵗ 5 Year Period:

	Departure	Year 1	Year 2	Year 3	Year 4	Year 5
	Previous Year	20% Growth ↑	21% Growth ↑	22% Growth ↑	23% Growth ↑	24% Growth ↑
1. Income	$350,000	$420,000	$508,200	$620,004	$762,605	$953,256
2.Profit Margin	25%	26%	27%	28%	29%	30%
3. Profit	$87,500	$109,200	$137,214	$173,601	$221,155	$285,977
Valuation	$350,000	$436,800	$548,856	$694,404	$884,622	$1,143,907

From the above projection table, in the next 5 years, Small Business Growth LLC has to generate $953,256 in income by year 5 to stay on track towards a profitable exit. John is a smart business owner, so he structured his business to have members instead just customers. Here is John's Income Model for the next 5 years:

Small Business Growth LLC
Income Model

Growth Factors	Departure Previous Year	Year 1 20% Growth	Year 2 21% Growth	Year 3 22% Growth	Year 4 23% Growth	Year 5 24% Growth
1.Leads	350	420	508	620	763	946
2.Conversion Rate	20%	20%	21%	22%	23%	24%
3.Members	70	84	107	136	175	227
4.Average # Months	10	10	10	10	10	10
5.Monthly Price	$500	$505	$510	$515	$520	$525
6.Income	$350,000	$424,200	$544,284	$702,465	$912,075	$1,191,494
7.Profit Margin	25%	26%	27%	28%	29%	30%
8.Profit	$87,500	$110,292	$146,156	$196,690	$264,502	$357,448
Valuation (4 x Profit)	$350,000	$441,168	$587,825	$786,760	$1,058,008	$1,429,793

Let us look the growth factors of Small Business Growth, LLC

1. Leads

The first growth factor is qualified leads are people who have a problem your business is currently solving. Without qualified leads, it is very difficult to grow a business.

Unfortunately, many business owners do not invest time to clearly define a qualified lead for their businesses and as a result, they waste some much time, energy and money chasing the unqualified leads.

To keep this simple, here is the qualified lead profile for Small Business Growth, LLC:

- Small business owner who has 2 or more employees, wants to grow their business consistently and have profitable exit in the next 5 – 10 years.

   With the simple profile above, it becomes easy for Small Business Growth, LLC to qualify businesses that are a good fit and disqualify businesses that are not a good fit.

   From the table above, Small Business Growth LLC had **350** leads in the pipeline or database and the company is expected to have 420 the following year.

2. Conversion Rate

The second growth factor is the conversion rate of a business enables a business to measure the percentage of leads who are becoming customers. From the table above, Small Business Growth LLC had a conversion rate of 20% in the previous year.

In effect 20% of the 350 leads generated became 70 members. Small Business Growth, LLC is projecting to have a conversion rate of 20% in year 1, 21% in year 2 and 24% by year 5.

The two most important factors that affect the conversion rate of a business are:

- **Quality of leads:** a business with quality leads in the database can easily increase its conversion rate.

- **Follow up:** Consistent follow up with qualified leads also increases the conversion rate

3. Average # of months

The third growth factor is the average number of months a member is retained in a business.

If your business does not yet have a membership program and has just customers, start tracking how many times in a year each customer buys a product or service from your business.

From the table above, the average number of months a member is expected to be retained at Small Business Growth LLC is 10 months. The longer the retention rate, the better.

If your business only deals with customers at this time, this is how you can calculate the average number of transactions. Assuming your business has 5 customers and each of them buys from you as follows, the average # of transactions in your business will be 5.

Customers	Number of Purchases In A Year
Customer A	7
Customer B	4
Customer C	5
Customer D	3
Customer E	6
Average # of Transactions (25 ÷ 5)	**5**

4. Monthly Price

The fourth growth factor is the monthly price. This is the price members of Small Business Growth LLC pay each month for the value they are receiving.

From the income model table above, the monthly price in the previous year was $500 and it is projected to increase by $5 each year until it reaches $525 in year 5.

It is always a good practice to increase the value you provide your members or customers before you increase the price.

If your business does not yet have a membership program and has just customers, start tracking the average price of your business.

For example, if your business has 3 products or services and the prices for product A, B and C are $100, $150 and $200 respectively, the average price will be the average:

$100 + $150 + $200 = ($450 ÷3) **$150**. The average price can increase if you increase the price of one of the products or vice versa.

If you only have one product or service, consider offering three different options to your members or customers to increase your average price.

For example, if you sell T-Shirts, instead of selling just 1 size at $20 for the small T-Shirt which means your average price will always be $20, consider adding a medium size T-shirt for $25 and a large size T-shirt for $30. Adding two sizes will raise your average price from $20 to $25.

If you sell services, instead of selling just 1 service at $500 which means your average price will always be $500, consider adding 2 more levels of services that provide additional value to your members or customers.

You can name the 3 levels of your services as Bronze $500, Silver $550 and Gold $600. Adding two levels of services will raise your average price from $5000 to $550.

Adopting the fourth growth factor of average price in your business impacts your profit greatly.

5. Profit Margin

The fifth growth factor is the profit margin. Simply defined, the profit margin is the percentage of income left after all the business expenses have been expended.

From the Income Model Table above, the profit margin for Small Business Growth LLC in the previous year was 25%. The profit margin is projected to increase each year from 26% in year 1 to 30% in year 5.

Managing expenses well is the keep to increasing the profit margin of a business. The lower the expenses, the more the profit margin.

Now that we have looked at the 5 growth factors using Small Business Growth LLC as our example, it is now time for you to answer some questions so you can create an Income Model for your business following some simple steps.

Once your business Income Model has been established, we can now proceed to establish some profitable growth habits for your business so you can increase your profit and grow your business towards a profitable exit.

Income Model Steps:

Step 1: Enter your 1st 5 years numbers into the table below:

The 1st 5 Year Period:

	Departure	Year 1	Year 2	Year 3	Year 4	Year 5
	Previous Year	___% Growth	___% Growth	___% Growth	___% Growth	___% Growth
1. Income						
2. Profit Margin						
3. Profit						
Valuation						

Step 2: Answer the questions below the table and use the answers to create your

Income Model

Income Model

Growth Factors	Departure	Year 1	Year 2	Year 3	Year 4	Year 5
	Previous Year	___% Growth	___% Growth	___% Growth	___% Growth	___% Growth
1.Leads						
2.Conversion Rate						
3.Members						
4.Average # Months						
5.Monthly Price						
6.Income						
7.Profit Margin						
8.Profit						
Valuation (4 x Profit)						

Questions

1. What is your business name? Write the name on the line above the words "Income Model."

4. What were your previous year's numbers? Enter them under the departure column. If you do not have previous year's numbers, leave the column blank.

5. How many leads do you need to reach your target profit number in year 1 and what are your projected growth rates from year 1 to year 5? Enter your growth rates and corresponding number of leads under each year accordingly.

6. What are your projected conversion rates from year 1 to year 5? Enter your conversion rates under each year accordingly.

7. Based on the number of leads you projected and your conversion rate, how many members or customers will you need to reach your profit target? Enter your numbers under each year accordingly.

8. What will your monthly or average price be from year 1 to 5? Enter your numbers under each year accordingly.

9. What is your projected income from year 1 to 5 based on the number of members or customers, average # of months or average number of transactions and monthly or average price? Your income for each year is a multiplication of the three numbers just mentioned. Drawing from the example of Small Business Growth LLC, the year 1 Income number is $424,200 (84 x 10 x $505). Enter your numbers under each year accordingly.

10. What are your projected profit margin percentages from year 1 to year 5? Enter your percentages under the corresponding years accordingly.

11. What are your profit numbers from year 1 to year 5? Enter your numbers under the corresponding year accordingly. Your profit is income x profit margin percentage. For the Small Business Growth LLC in year 1, the number is $110,292 ($441,168 x 26%).

12. What is the projected value of your business from year 1 to year 5? Enter your numbers under the corresponding year accordingly. Value is 4 x profit. For the Small Business Growth LLC in year 1, the number is $441,168 ($110,292 x 4).

Now that you have created your Income Model, it is time to establish your quarterly map and weekly customer or member projections.

We are going to start this process using the Small Business Growth LLC example again. Let us get started on the next page:

Quarterly Maps

Step 1: Established Income Model

To establish quarterly maps for Small Business Growth, LLC, let us start with its Income Model previously established:

Small Business Growth LLC
Income Model

Growth Factors	Departure Previous Year	Year 1 20% Growth	Year 2 21% Growth	Year 3 22% Growth	Year 4 23% Growth	Year 5 24% Growth
1.Leads	350	420	508	620	763	938
2.Conversion Rate	20%	20%	21%	22%	23%	24%
3.Members	70	84	107	136	175	225
4.Average # Months	10	10	10	10	10	10
5.Monthly Price	$500	$505	$510	$515	$520	$525
6.Income	$350,000	$424,200	$544,282	$702,465	$912,075	$1,181,885
7.Profit Margin	25%	26%	27%	28%	29%	30%
8.Profit	$87,500	$110,292	$146,956	$196,690	$264,502	$354,566
Valuation (4 x Profit)	$350,000	$441,168	$548,856	$694,404	$884,620	$1,143,908

Step 2: Break Year 1 Projections Into 4 Quarters

The 2ⁿᵈ step in this process is to break the 1ˢᵗ year projection into 4 quarters as shown below:

Growth Factors	Departure	Q1	Q 2	Q3	Q 4	Destination
1.Leads	350	63	84	126	147	420
2.Conversion Rate	20%	20%	20%	20%	20%	20%
3.Members	70	13	17	25	29	84
4.Average # Months	10	10	10	10	10	10
5.Monthly Price	$500	$505	$505	$505	$505	$505
6.Income	$350,000	$63,630	$84,840	$127,260	$148,470	$424,200
7.Profit Margin	25%	26%	26%	26%	26%	26%
8.Profit	$87,500	$16,544	$22,058	$33,088	$38,602	$110,292
Percentages		15%	20%	30%	35%	100%

Let us look at each column:

- **Departure:** The departure column from the table above is simply a representation of previous year's numbers.

- **Destination:** The destination column shows the total numbers of year 1's projection.

- **Q1:** These numbers represent 15% of the total numbers shown under the destination column.

- **Q2:** These numbers represent 20% of the total numbers shown under the destination column.

- **Q3:** These numbers represent 30% of the total numbers shown under the destination column.

- **Q4:** These numbers represent 35% of the total numbers shown under the destination column.

Starting with a small percentage 15% in Q1 and increasing the percentages to 35% in Q4 enables any business to build momentum throughout the year.

Step 3: Quarterly Membership Budget

To establish a quarterly membership budget for Small Business Growth, LLC, we will focus on two growth factors; leads and conversion rate. Consistent lead generation and follow-up will automatically increase the number of members.

The table below shows the membership budget for the 1st quarter:

Growth Factors	W1	W2	W3	W4	W5	W6	W7	W8	W9	W10	W11	W12	W13	Total
1.Leads	5	5	5	5	5	5	5	5	5	5	5	5	5	65
2.Conversion %	20	20	20	20	20	20	20	20	20	20	20	20	20	20%
3.Members	1	1	1	1	1	1	1	1	1	1	1	1	1	13

How did we arrive at the Q1 numbers above?

- **Leads:** We simply divided the Q1 projection of 63 leads by 13. 63 ÷ 13 = 4.85. Since we cannot fraction people, we will round up 4.85 to 5. Hence 5 x 13 = 65.

- **Conversion Rate:** The projected conversion rate is 20%. So, 5 x 20% = 1

- **Members:** 1 member a week for 13 weeks gives us 13 members by the end of Q1

Growth Factors	W1	W2	W3	W4	W5	W6	W7	W8	W9	W10	W11	W12	W13	Total
1.Leads	6	6	6	6	6	6	6	6	6	6	6	6	6	78
2.Conversion %	20	20	20	20	20	20	20	20	20	20	20	20	20	20%
3.Members	1	1	1	1	1	1	1	1	1	1	1	1	1	13

How did we arrive at the Q2 numbers above?

1. **Leads:** We simply divided the Q2 projection of 84 leads by 13. 84 ÷ 13 = 6.46. Since we cannot fraction people, we will round down 6.46 to 6. Hence 6 x 13 = 78.

2. **Conversion Rate:** The projected conversion rate is 20%. So, 6 x 20% = 1.2 rounded down to 1

3. **Members:** 1 member a week for 13 weeks gives us 13 members by the end of Q2

Growth Factors	W1	W2	W3	W4	W5	W6	W7	W8	W9	W10	W11	W12	W13	Total
1.Leads	10	10	10	10	10	10	10	10	10	10	10	10	10	130
2.Conversion	20	20	20	20	20	20	20	20	20	20	20	20	20	20%
3.Members	2	2	2	2	2	2	2	2	2	2	2	2	2	26

How did we arrive at the Q3 numbers above?

1. **Leads**: We simply divided the Q3 projection of 126 leads by 13. 126 ÷ 13 = 9.69. Since we cannot fraction people, we will round up 9.69 to 10. Hence 10 x 13 = 130.

2. **Conversion Rate:** The projected conversion rate is 20%. So, 10 x 20% = 2

3. **Members**: 2 members a week for 13 weeks gives us 26 members by the end of Q3

Growth Factors	W1	W2	W3	W4	W5	W6	W7	W8	W9	W10	W11	W12	W13	Total
1.Leads	12	12	12	12	12	12	12	12	12	12	12	12	12	156
2.Conversion	20	20	20	20	20	20	20	20	20	20	20	20	20	20%
3.Members	3	3	3	3	3	3	3	3	3	3	3	3	3	39

How did we arrive at the Q4 numbers above?

1. **Leads**: We simply divided the Q4 projection of 147 leads by 13. 147 ÷ 13 = 11.30 Since we cannot fraction people, we will round up 11.30 to 12. Hence 12 x 13 = 156.

2. **Conversion Rate:** The projected conversion rate is 20%. So, 12 x 20% = 2.4 rounded up to 3.

3. **Members**: 3 members a week for 13 weeks gives us 39 members by the end of Q4

We decided to round up the 4th quarter numbers to enable us budget accurately. Let's add the expected number of members from the four quarters and verify them with the 1st year's projection above.

Membership Verification Table

Projections	Q1	Q2	Q3	Q4	Total
Year 1	13	17	25	29	84
Quarterly	13	13	26	39	91

As we can see from the above table, the quarterly budget number is 91 and the year projection number is 84. This verifies that we have budgeted appropriately. At the end of the year, if the actual number of members is 91, Small Business Growth LLC will actually make more income and profit.

However, if the quarterly budget number was below the year 1 projection number, we will revise the budget until the quarterly budget number is equal or more that the year's projected number.

Now it is your turn to follow Small Business Growth's example and establish project the next year and establish a quarterly budget for leads, conversion rate and number of members or customers.

Your Quarterly Maps

Step 1: Established Income Model

Complete the table below with your previously established Income Model:

_____

Income Model

	Departure	Year 1	Year 2	Year 3	Year 4	Year 5
Growth Factors	Previous Year	___% Growth	___% Growth	___% Growth	___% Growth	___% Growth
1.Leads						
2.Conversion Rate						
3.Members						
4.Average # Months						
5.Monthly Price						
6.Income						
7.Profit Margin						
8.Profit						
Valuation (4 x Profit)						

Step 2: Break Year 1 Projections Into 4 Quarters

The 2nd step in this process is to break the 1st year projection into 4 quarters and use the results to complete the table below:

Growth Factors	Departure	Q1	Q 2	Q3	Q 4	Destination
1.Leads						
2.Conversion Rate						
3.Members						
4.Average # Months						
5.Monthly Price						
6.Income						
7.Profit Margin						
8.Profit						
Percentages		____%	____%	____%	____%	100%

Let us look at each of your columns:

- **Departure**: The departure column from the table above should simply be a representation of your previous year's numbers. If you do not have previous year's numbers, leave the departure column blank.

- **Destination**: The destination column shows the total numbers of your year 1's projection.

- **Q1**: These numbers represent ____% of the total numbers shown under the destination column. You should choose the percentage you desire to start with. We recommend you start with a smaller percentage such as 10% or 15% and build the momentum as the year matures towards the fourth quarter.

- **Q2**: These numbers represent ____% of the total numbers shown under the destination column.

- **Q3**: These numbers represent ____% of the total numbers shown under the destination column.

- **Q4**: These numbers represent ____% of the total numbers shown under the destination column.

Step 3: Quarterly Membership Budget

To establish a quarterly membership or customer budget for your business, you need to focus on two growth factors; leads and conversion rate. Consistent lead generation and follow-up will automatically increase the number of members or customers.

Complete the table below with your Q1 membership or customer budget:

Growth Factors	W1	W2	W3	W4	W5	W6	W7	W8	W9	W10	W11	W12	W13	Total
1.Leads														
2.Conversion														___%
3.Members														

How should you calculate your Q1 members or customer numbers?

- **Leads**: Simply divide the Q1 projection of ____ leads by 13. ____ ÷ 13 = ____. If the number ends with a fraction, round the number up or down ____ to ____.

- Hence ____ x ____ = ____.

- **Conversion Rate**: Use your projected conversion rate of ____%. So, ____ x ____% = ____

- **Members/Customers**: ____member(s)/customer(s) a week for 13 weeks gives us ____ members/customers by the end of Q1

Growth Factors	W1	W2	W3	W4	W5	W6	W7	W8	W9	W10	W11	W12	W13	Total
1.Leads														
2.Conversion														___%
3.Members														

How should you calculate your Q2 members or customer numbers?

- **Leads**: Simply divide the Q2 projection of ____ leads by 13. ____ ÷ 13 = ____. If the number ends with a fraction, round the number up or down ____ to ____.

- Hence ____ x ____ = ____.

- **Conversion Rate:** Use your projected conversion rate of ____%. So, ____ x ____% = ____

- **Members/Customers**: _____ member(s)/customer(s) a week for 13 weeks gives us _____ members/customers by the end of Q2

Growth Factors	W1	W2	W3	W4	W5	W6	W7	W8	W9	W10	W11	W12	W13	Total
1.Leads														
2.Conversion														___%
3.Members														

How should you calculate your Q3 members or customer numbers?

- **Leads**: Simply divide the Q3 projection of _____ leads by 13. _____ ÷ 13 = _____. If the number ends with a fraction, round the number up or down _____ to _____.

- Hence _____ x _____ = _____.

- **Conversion Rate:** Use your projected conversion rate of _____%. So, _____ x _____% = _____

- **Members/Customers**: _____ member(s)/customer(s) a week for 13 weeks gives us _____ members/customers by the end of Q3.

Growth Factors	W1	W2	W3	W4	W5	W6	W7	W8	W9	W10	W11	W12	W13	Total
1.Leads														
2.Conversion														___%
3.Members														

How should you calculate your Q4 members or customer numbers?

- **Leads**: Simply divide the Q4 projection of _____ leads by 13. _____ ÷ 13 = _____. If the number ends with a fraction, round the number up or down _____ to _____.

- Hence _____ x _____ = _____.

- **Conversion Rate:** Use your projected conversion rate of _____%. So, _____ x _____% = _____

- **Members/Customers**: _____ member(s)/customer(s) a week for 13 weeks gives us _____ members/customers by the end of Q4

Membership or Customer Verification Table

Projections	Q1	Q2	Q3	Q4	Total
Year 1					
Quarterly					

Is your quarterly budget total number equal or greater than your year's projected number? If your answer is no, revise your quarterly budget numbers until the total is equal or greater than your year's projection.

Now that you have completed your year's projection and quarterly maps, let us proceed to establish some profitable growth routines.

STEP 4
PROFITABLE GROWTH ROUTINES

To keep this simple, we will still focus on two growth factors; leads and conversion rate. The key to higher conversion rates is consistent follow-up.

Therefore, we will use consistent leads and consistent follow-up to establish growth routines. Again, we will use Small Business Growth LLC as our example.

Let us use the following 5 steps to establish the consistent lead generation and followup routines for Small Business Growth LLC.

Step 1: List of Media Channels

Here are the viable media channels for Small Business Growth LLC:

1. Referrals

2. Events - Celebrations, planning

3. Networking

4. Direct Mail

5. Social Media

6. Print/News Paper ads

7. Radio/Television

8. Text/Email

9. E-Newsletters/Print Newsletters

10. Joint Ventures

11. Billboards

12. Telemarketing

Step 2: Select 5 Viable Media Channels

Why 5? Identifying 5 viable media channels will help Small Business Growth LLC stay focused on a few channels so they can deploy them consistently throughout the year.

Due Small Business Growth LLC's ideal target member – market profile, the following media channels will be viable since the ideal target member can be reached through these media channels profitably.

1. Texts and/or Social Media

2. Emails and Referrals

3. Newsletter/Cards

4. Celebrations

5. Planning

Step 3: Establish a routine for each media channel using the 5 routines framework

The 5 routines are:

1. Daily Routine

2. Weekly Routine

3. Monthly Routine

4. Quarterly Routine

5. Yearly Routine

Let's establish them one by one:

Daily Routines

Small Business Growth LLC will use **text** messages and/or **social media** to generate leads and follow-up daily.

Weekly Routines

Small Business Growth LLC will use **emails** and ask for **referrals** to generate leads and follow-up weekly.

Monthly Routines

Small Business Growth LLC will use **events** such as workshops and webinars and **newsletters** to generate leads and follow-up monthly.

Quarterly Routines

Small Business Growth LLC will use **events** such as quarterly celebrations to generate leads and follow-up quarterly.

Yearly Routines

Small Business Growth LLC will use **events** such as yearly planning and celebrations such as Thanksgiving, Christmas and new year to generate leads and follow-up yearly.

Step 4: Create A Lead Generation & Follow-up Calendar

Here is Small Business Growth LLC example:

Media/Routines	1. Daily	2. Weekly	3. Monthly	4. Quarterly	5. Yearly
1. Texts/Social Media	✓	✓	✓	✓	✓
2. Referrals/Emails		✓	✓	✓	✓
3. Newsletter/Cards			✓	✓	✓
4. Celebrations			✓	✓	✓
5. Planning				✓	✓

Step 5: Budget Time For Consistent Lead Generation And Follow-up

The time you budget depends on how many people are involved in lead generation in your business and how much money you invest into your lead generation efforts.

Small Business Growth, LLC plans to invest 120 minutes or 2 hours each day and an extra 60 minutes each week on Wednesdays towards leads generation and follow-up.

Growth Factor	Monday	Tuesday	Wednesday	Thursday	Friday	Weekly Total
Leads	90	90	180	90	90	540
Follow-up	90	90	90	90	90	450
Daily/Weekly Total	180	180	270	180	180	990

Now is your turn that we have used Small Business Growth, LLC's example to demonstrate, now it is your turn. Follow the steps below to create your profitable growth routines.

Your Profitable Growth Routines

Step 1: List of Media Channels

Here are some media channels. You can add more to the list below:

- Referrals

- Events

- Networking

- Direct Mail

- Social Media

- Print/News Paper ads

- Radio/Television

- Text/Email

- E-Newsletters/Print Newsletters

- Joint Ventures

- Billboards

- Telemarketing

- _____

- _____

- _____

Step 2: Select 5 Viable Media Channels

Why 5? Identifying 5 viable media channels will enable your business stay focused on a few channels so you can deploy them consistently throughout the year.

Your ideal target member – market profile, should influence your choice of media. What 5 media channels will you focus on? List them below:

- _____

- _____

- _____

- _____

- _____

Step 3: Establish a routine for each media channel using the 5 routines framework

The 5 routines are:

- Daily Routine

- Weekly Routine

- Monthly Routine

- Quarterly Routine

- Yearly Routine

Let's establish them one by one:

Daily Routines

_____will use _____ messages and/or _____ to generate leads and follow-up daily.

Weekly Routines

_____ will use _____ and ask for **referrals** to generate leads and follow-up weekly.

Monthly Routines

_____will use _____ such as _____ and/or to generate leads and follow-up monthly.

Quarterly Routines

_____will use _____ such as quarterly celebrations to generate leads and follow-up quarterly.

Yearly Routines

_____ will use _____ such as yearly planning and celebrations such as Thanksgiving, Christmas and new year to generate leads and follow-up yearly.

Step 4: Create Your Lead Generation & Follow-up Calendar

Use the table below to create your lead generation and follow-up calendar:

Media/Routines	1. Daily	2. Weekly	3. Monthly	4. Quarterly	5. Yearly
	✓	✓	✓	✓	✓
		✓	✓	✓	✓
			✓	✓	✓
				✓	✓
					✓

Step 5: Budget Time For Your Consistent Lead Generation And Follow-up

The time you budget depends on how many people are involved in lead generation in your business and how much money you invest into your lead generation efforts.

Use the table below to determine how many minutes will be invested each day in your business to consistently generate leads and follow-up.

Growth Factor	Monday	Tuesday	Wednesday	Thursday	Friday	Weekly Total
Leads						
Follow-up						
Daily/Weekly Total						

Now that you have your routines established, let us proceed to talk about accountability.

STEP 5
ACCOUNTABILITY

The American Society of Training and Development (ASTD) did a study on accountability and found that you have a **65%** chance of completing a goal if you commit to someone.

But you can increase that **likelihood of success to 95%** if you have an 'accountability appointment' with the person you committed to. The more layers of accountability you establish in your business, the more profitable your business will become.

Again, let us use Small Business Growth LLC's example to demonstrate following these 5 steps:

Step 1: Establish accountability routines using the 5 routines framework

The 5 routines are:

- Daily Accountability Routine

- Weekly Accountability Routine

- Monthly Accountability Routine

- Quarterly Accountability Routine

- Yearly Accountability Routine

Let's establish them one by one:

Daily Accountability

Small Business Growth LLC will focus on consistency rate as a daily accountability measure.

When we established daily and weekly growth routines for Small Business Growth LLC, we also budgeted time as follows:

Growth Factors	Monday	Tuesday	Wednesday	Thursday	Friday	Weekly Total
Leads	90	90	180	90	90	**540**
Follow-up	90	90	90	90	90	**450**
Daily/Weekly Total	180	180	270	180	180	**990**

Consistency Rate is simply a measure of the budgeted time compared to the actual time invested expressed as a percentage.

Growth Factors	Monday	Tuesday	Wednesday	Thursday	Friday	Weekly
Budget (B)	180	180	270	180	180	**990**
Actual (A)	180	180	200	180	120	**860**
Consistency Rate: A/B	100%	100%	74%	100%	66%	**86%**

Based on the above the weekly consistency rate average is 86%. A consistency rate less than 80% in a week is a sign the business is getting off track.

Weekly Accountability

Small Business Growth LLC will conversion rate as a weekly accountability measure.

When we established the quarterly membership/customer budgets for Small Business Growth LLC, we established the following for the 1st quarter:

Growth Factors	W1	W2	W3	W4	W5	W6	W7	W8	W9	W10	W11	W12	W13	Total
1.Leads	5	5	5	5	5	5	5	5	5	5	5	5	5	65
2.Conversion	20	20	20	20	20	20	20	20	20	20	20	20	20	20%
3.Members	1	1	1	1	1	1	1	1	1	1	1	1	1	13

Conversion Rate is simply a measure of the number of members or customers divided by the number of leads actually generated expressed as a percentage.

Growth Factor	Monday	Tuesday	Wednesday	Thursday	Friday	Weekly
Leads (L)	1	1	1	1	1	**5**
Members (M)	0	0	0	1	0	**1**
Conversion Rate: M/L	0%	0%	0%	100%	0%	**20%**

Based on the above table, the weekly conversion rate average is 20%. This number is in line with the budgeted results. If the results were higher or lower than the budgeted results, we need to know why so we can stay on track to achieve our profit goal.

Monthly Accountability

Small Business Growth LLC will focus on Financial Statements for monthly accountability.

Quarterly Accountability

Small Business Growth LLC will focus on quarterly review and preview for quarterly accountability.

Yearly Accountability

Small Business Growth LLC will focus yearly planning - Projections and taxes for yearly accountability.

Step 2: Create An Accountability Calendar

Here is Small Business Growth LLC example:

Accountability	1. Daily	2. Weekly	3. Monthly	4. Quarterly	5. Yearly
Consistency Rate	✓	✓	✓	✓	✓
Conversion Rate		✓	✓	✓	✓
Financial Statements			✓	✓	✓
Quarterly Reviews				✓	✓
Planning					✓

Step 3: Budget Time For Consistent Accountability

The time you budget depends on how long you want your accountability meetings to last. See Small Business Growth, LLC example below. Time in the table below is in minutes.

Accountability	1. Daily	2. Weekly	3. Monthly	4. Quarterly	5. Yearly
Consistency Rate	5 - 10				
Conversion Rate		30 - 45			
Financial Statements			60 -70		
Quarterly Reviews				90 - 120	
Planning					300 - 540

Now that we have used Small Business Growth LLC's example to demonstrate, it is your turn to establish your consistent accountability schedule. Questions and templates have been provided to make this process easy to complete.

Follow the 5 steps below to establish your accountability routines:

Step 1: Establish accountability routines using the 5 routines framework

The 5 routines are:

- Daily Accountability Routine

- Weekly Accountability Routine

- Monthly Accountability Routine

- Quarterly Accountability Routine

- Yearly Accountability Routine

- Let's establish them one by one:

Your Daily Accountability

Your daily accountability measure should be focused on consistency rate to stay on track.

Use your previously budgeted time to complete tables below:

Growth Factor	Monday	Tuesday	Wednesday	Thursday	Friday	Weekly Total
Leads						
Follow-up						
Daily/Weekly Total						

Consistency Rate is simply a measure of the budgeted time compared to the actual time invested expressed as a percentage.

Growth Factor	Monday	Tuesday	Wednesday	Thursday	Friday	Weekly
Budget (B)						
Actual (A)						
Consistency Rate: A/B	____%	____%	____%	____%	____%	____%

A consistency rate less than 80% in a week is a sign the business is getting off track.

Your Weekly Accountability

Your conversion rate should be your weekly accountability measure.

Use your 1st quarter's numbers previously established to complete the template below:

Growth Factors	W1	W2	W3	W4	W5	W6	W7	W8	W9	W10	W11	W12	W13	Total
1.Leads														
2.Conversion %														
3.Members														

Conversion Rate is simply a measure of the number of members or customers divided by the number of leads actually generated expressed as a percentage.

Growth Factor	Monday	Tuesday	Wednesday	Thursday	Friday	Weekly
Leads (L)	1	1	1	1	1	**5**
Members (M)	0	0	0	1	0	**1**
Conversion Rate: M/L	0%	0%	0%	100%	0%	20%

Based on the above table, the weekly conversion rate average is 20%. This number is in line with the budgeted results. If the results were higher or lower than the budgeted results, we need to know why so we can stay on track to achieve our profit goal.

More templates have been provided in the accountability template section of this workbook so you can keep track of your progress weekly.

Your Monthly Accountability

You should focus on using your Financial Statements for your monthly accountability.

Your Quarterly Accountability

You should focus on using quarterly review and preview for your quarterly accountability.

Your Yearly Accountability

You should focus on yearly planning - Projections and taxes for your yearly accountability.

Step 2: Create An Accountability Calendar

Based on the above recommendations, your accountability calendar should be as follows:

Accountability	1. Daily	2. Weekly	3. Monthly	4. Quarterly	5. Yearly
Consistency Rate	✓	✓	✓	✓	✓
Conversion Rate		✓	✓	✓	✓
Financial Statements			✓	✓	✓
Quarterly Reviews				✓	✓
Planning					✓

Step 3: Budget Time For Consistent Accountability

The time you budget depends on how long you want your accountability meetings to last. Enter the answers to the following questions in the table below:

- How many minutes will you invest to review your consistency rate each day?

- How many minutes will you invest to hold your weekly accountability meeting?

- How many minutes will you invest to hold your monthly accountability meeting?

- How many minutes will you invest to hold your quarterly accountability meeting?

- How many minutes will you invest towards your yearly planning meeting?

Accountability	1. Daily	2. Weekly	3. Monthly	4. Quarterly	5. Yearly
Consistency Rate					
Conversion Rate					
Financial Statements					
Quarterly Reviews					
Planning					

Quarterly Maps Bonus

Your Quarterly Maps

Step 1: Established Income Model

Complete the table below with your previously established Income Model:

Income Model

Growth Factors	Departure Previous Year	Year 1 ___% Growth	Year 2 ___% Growth	Year 3 ___% Growth	Year 4 ___% Growth	Year 5 ___% Growth
1.Leads						
2.Conversion Rate						
3.Members						
4.Average # Months						
5.Monthly Price						
6.Income						
7.Profit Margin						
8.Profit						
Valuation (4 x Profit)						

Step 2: Break Year 1 Projections Into 4 Quarters

The 2nd step in this process is to break the 1st year projection into 4 quarters and use the results to complete the table below:

Growth Factors	Departure	Q1	Q 2	Q3	Q 4	Destination
1.Leads						
2.Conversion Rate						
3.Members						
4.Average # Months						
5.Monthly Price						

6.Income					
7.Profit Margin					
8.Profit					
Percentages		____%	____%	____%	____%	100%

Let us look at each of your columns:

- **Departure**: The departure column from the table above should simply be a representation of your previous year's numbers. If you do not have previous year's numbers, leave the departure column blank.

- **Destination**: The destination column shows the total numbers of your year 1's projection.

- **Q1**: These numbers represent ____% of the total numbers shown under the destination column. You should choose the percentage you desire to start with. We recommend you start with a smaller percentage such as 10% or 15% and build the momentum as the year matures towards the fourth quarter.

- **Q2**: These numbers represent ____% of the total numbers shown under the destination column.

- **Q3**: These numbers represent ____% of the total numbers shown under the destination column.

- **Q4**: These numbers represent ____% of the total numbers shown under the destination column.

Step 3: Quarterly Membership Budget

To establish a quarterly membership or customer budget for your business, you need to focus on two growth factors; leads and conversion rate. Consistent lead generation and follow-up will automatically increase the number of members or customers.

Complete the table below with your Q1 membership or customer budget:

Growth Factors	W1	W2	W3	W4	W5	W6	W7	W8	W9	W10	W11	W12	W13	Total
1.Leads														
2.Conversion														____%
3.Members														

How should you calculate your Q1 members or customer numbers?

- **Leads**: Simply divide the Q1 projection of ____ leads by 13. ____ ÷ 13 = ____. If the number ends with a fraction, round the number up or down ____ to ____.

  Hence ____ x ____ = ____.

- **Conversion Rate**: Use your projected conversion rate of ____%. So, ____ x ____% = ____

- **Members/Customers**: ____member(s)/customer(s) a week for 13 weeks gives us ____ members/customers by the end of Q1

Growth Factors	W1	W2	W3	W4	W5	W6	W7	W8	W9	W10	W11	W12	W13	Total
1.Leads														
2.Conversion														___%
3.Members														

How should you calculate your Q2 members or customer numbers?

- **Leads**: Simply divide the Q2 projection of _____ leads by 13. _____ ÷ 13 = _____. If the number ends with a fraction, round the number up or down _____ to _____.

  Hence _____ x _____ = _____.

- **Conversion Rate:** Use your projected conversion rate of _____%. So, _____ x _____% = _____

- **Members/Customers:** _____ member(s)/customer(s) a week for 13 weeks gives us _____ members/customers by the end of Q2

Growth Factors	W1	W2	W3	W4	W5	W6	W7	W8	W9	W10	W11	W12	W13	Total
1.Leads														
2.Conversion														___%
3.Members														

How should you calculate your Q3 members or customer numbers?

- **Leads**: Simply divide the Q3 projection of _____ leads by 13. _____ ÷ 13 = _____. If the number ends with a fraction, round the number up or down _____ to _____. Hence _____ x _____ = _____.

- **Conversion Rate:** Use your projected conversion rate of _____%. So, _____ x _____% = _____

- **Members/Customers:** _____ member(s)/customer(s) a week for 13 weeks gives us _____ members/customers by the end of Q3.

Growth Factors	W1	W2	W3	W4	W5	W6	W7	W8	W9	W10	W11	W12	W13	Total
1.Leads														
2.Conversion														___%
3.Members														

How should you calculate your Q4 members or customer numbers?

- **Leads**: Simply divide the Q4 projection of _____ leads by 13. _____ ÷ 13 = _____. If the number ends with a fraction, round the number up or down _____ to _____.

  Hence _____ x _____ = _____.

- **Conversion Rate**: Use your projected conversion rate of _____%. So, _____ x _____% = _____

- **Members/Customers**: _____member(s)/customer(s) a week for 13 weeks gives us _____ members/customers by the end of Q4

Membership or Customer Verification Table

Projections	Q1	Q2	Q3	Q4	Total
Year 1					
Quarterly					

Is your quarterly budget total number equal or greater than your year's projected number? If your answer is no, revise your quarterly budget numbers until the total is equal or greater than your year's projection.

Now that you have completed your year's projection and quarterly maps, let us proceed to establish some profitable growth routines.

Accountability Scoreboard Templates

In the accountability section above, we recommended you design and establish a daily, weekly, monthly, quarterly and yearly accountability system in your business so you can navigate towards a profitable exit.

In this section, we want to provide you with scoreboard templates you can use to record your results and make improvements as you navigate your business towards a profitable exit.

Weekly Consistency Rate Scoreboard

Consistency Rate is simply a measure of the budgeted time compared to the actual time invested expressed as a percentage as exemplified below.

Growth Factors	Monday	Tuesday	Wednesday	Thursday	Friday	Weekly
Budget (B)	180	180	270	180	180	990
Actual (A)	180	180	200	180	120	860
Consistency Rate: A/B	100%	100%	74%	100%	66%	86%

A consistency rate less than 80% in a week is a sign the business is getting off track.

Weekly Conversion Rate Scoreboard

Conversion Rate is simply a measure of the number of members or customers divided by the number of leads actually generated expressed as a percentage as exemplified below.

Growth Factor	Monday	Tuesday	Wednesday	Thursday	Friday	Weekly
Leads (L)	1	1	1	1	1	**5**
Members (M)	0	0	0	1	0	**1**
Conversion Rate: M/L	0%	0%	0%	100%	0%	20%

Quarterly Scoreboard

The quarterly scoreboard is used to capture your consistency rate and conversion rate as a weekly summary so we can see at a glance the scores of your business on a quarterly basis as exemplified below:

Growth Factors	W1	W2	W3	W4	W5	W6	W7	W8	W9	W10	W11	W12	W13	Tot/Ave
Consistency %	88	70	90	80	60	100	80	90	70	80	90	100	100	84%
Leads	5	8	6	4	5	3	5	2	5	6	7	4	5	65
Members	1	1	2	1	1	2	2	3	1	1	1	1	1	18
Conversion	20	13	33	25	20	65	40	150	20	17	14	25	20	36%

Weekly Consistency Rate Scoreboard Example

Monday 1/6/20								
	Budgeted Time		**Growth Factors**	**Actual Time**			**Time In Minutes**	
	Start	End	Budgeted Activity	Start	End	Actual Activity	Budget	Actual
1	10:00am	11:00 am	Leads	10:00am	11:00 am	Leads	60	60
2	11:00am	11:30 am	Follow-up	11:00am	11:20 am	Follow-up	30	20
Total							90	80
Consistency Rate: Total Actual (A)/Budget (B)							88%	

Tuesday 1/7/20								
	Budgeted Time		Growth Factors	Actual Time			Time In Minutes	
	Start	End	Budgeted Activity	Start	End	Actual Activity	Budget	Actual
1	10:00am	11:00 am	Leads	10:00am	11:00 am	Leads	60	60
2	11:00am	11:30 am	Follow-up	11:00am	11:20 am	Follow-up	30	20
Total							90	80
Consistency Rate: Total Actual (A)/Budget (B)							88%	

Wednesday 1/8/20								
	Budgeted Time		Growth Factors	Actual Time			Time In Minutes	
	Start	End	Budgeted Activity	Start	End	Actual Activity	Budget	Actual
1	10:00am	11:00 am	Leads	10:00am	11:00 am	Leads	60	60
2	11:00am	11:30 am	Follow-up	11:00am	11:20 am	Follow-up	30	20
Total							90	80
Consistency Rate: Total Actual (A)/Budget (B)							88%	

Thursday 1/9/20								
	Budgeted Time		Growth Factors	Actual Time			Time In Minutes	
	Start	End	Budgeted Activity	Start	End	Actual Activity	Budget	Actual
1	10:00am	11:00 am	Leads	10:00am	11:00 am	Leads	60	60
2	11:00am	11:30 am	Follow-up	11:00am	11:20 am	Follow-up	30	20
Total							90	80

Consistency Rate: Total Actual (A)/Budget (B)							88%	

Friday 1/10/20

	Budgeted Time		Growth Factors	Actual Time			Time In Minutes	
	Start	End	Budgeted Activity	Start	End	Actual Activity	Budget	Actual
1	10:00am	11:00 am	Leads	10:00am	11:00 am	Leads	60	60
2	11:00am	11:30 am	Follow-up	11:00am	11:20 am	Follow-up	30	20
Total							90	80
Consistency Rate: Total Actual (A)/Budget (B)							88%	

Weekly Conversion Rate Scoreboard Example

Conversion Rate is simply a measure of the number of members or customers divided by the number of leads actually generated expressed as a percentage as exemplified below.

Growth Factor	Monday	Tuesday	Wednesday	Thursday	Friday	Weekly
Leads (L)	1	1	1	1	1	**5**
Members (M)	0	0	0	1	0	**1**
Conversion Rate: M/L	0%	0%	0%	100%	0%	20%

Quarterly Scoreboard Example

The quarterly scoreboard is used to capture your consistency rate and conversion rate as a weekly summary so we can see at a glance the scores of your business on a quarterly basis as exemplified below:

Growth Factors	W1	W2	W3	W4	W5	W6	W7	W8	W9	W10	W11	W12	W13	Tot/Ave
Consistency	88	70	90	80	60	100	80	90	70	80	90	100	100	84%
Leads	5	8	6	4	5	3	5	2	5	6	7	4	5	65
Members	1	1	2	1	1	2	2	3	1	1	1	1	1	18
Conversion	20	13	33	25	20	65	40	150	20	17	14	25	20	36%

Q1 Accountability Scoreboard Templates

Consistency Rate Scoreboard – Week 1

Monday: _____

	Budgeted Time		Growth Factors	Actual Time			Time In Minutes	
	Start	End	Budgeted Activity	Start	End	Actual Activity	Budget	Actual
1			Leads			Leads		
2			Follow-up			Follow-up		
Total								

Consistency Rate: Total Actual (A)/Budget (B)

Tuesday: _____

	Budgeted Time		Growth Factors	Actual Time			Time In Minutes	
	Start	End	Budgeted Activity	Start	End	Actual Activity	Budget	Actual
1			Leads			Leads		
2			Follow-up			Follow-up		
Total								

Consistency Rate: Total Actual (A)/Budget (B)

Wednesday: _____

	Budgeted Time		Growth Factors	Actual Time			Time In Minutes	
	Start	End	Budgeted Activity	Start	End	Actual Activity	Budget	Actual
1			Leads			Leads		
2			Follow-up			Follow-up		
Total								

Consistency Rate: Total Actual (A)/Budget (B)

Thursday: _____

	Budgeted Time		Growth Factors	Actual Time			Time In Minutes	
	Start	End	Budgeted Activity	Start	End	Actual Activity	Budget	Actual
1			Leads			Leads		
2			Follow-up			Follow-up		
Total								

	Consistency Rate: Total Actual (A)/Budget (B)							
Friday: _____								
	Budgeted Time		Growth Factors	Actual Time			Time In Minutes	
	Start	End	Budgeted Activity	Start	End	Actual Activity	Budget	Actual
1	10:00am	11:00 am	Leads	10:00am	11:00 am	Leads		
2	11:00am	11:30 am	Follow-up	11:00am	11:20 am	Follow-up		
Total								
	Consistency Rate: Total Actual (A)/Budget (B)							

Conversion Rate Scoreboard

Growth Factor	Monday	Tuesday	Wednesday	Thursday	Friday	Week 2
Leads (L)						
Members (M)						
Conversion Rate: M/L						

Quarterly Scoreboard

Pull from week 1 above. The average from Monday to Friday

Growth Factors	W1	W2	W3	W4	W5	W6	W7	W8	W9	W10	W11	W12	W13	Ave/Tot
Consistency %														
Leads														
Members														
Conversion %														

Consistency Rate Scoreboard – Week 2

Monday: _____								
	Budgeted Time		Growth Factors	Actual Time			Time In Minutes	
	Start	End	Budgeted Activity	Start	End	Actual Activity	Budget	Actual
1			Leads			Leads		
2			Follow-up			Follow-up		
Total								

Consistency Rate: Total Actual (A)/Budget (B)									

Tuesday: _____

	Budgeted Time		Growth Factors	Actual Time				Time In Minutes	
	Start	End	Budgeted Activity	Start	End	Actual Activity		Budget	Actual
1			Leads			Leads			
2			Follow-up			Follow-up			
Total									

Consistency Rate: Total Actual (A)/Budget (B)									

Wednesday: _____

	Budgeted Time		Growth Factors	Actual Time				Time In Minutes	
	Start	End	Budgeted Activity	Start	End	Actual Activity		Budget	Actual
1			Leads			Leads			
2			Follow-up			Follow-up			
Total									

Consistency Rate: Total Actual (A)/Budget (B)									

Thursday: _____

	Budgeted Time		Growth Factors	Actual Time				Time In Minutes	
	Start	End	Budgeted Activity	Start	End	Actual Activity		Budget	Actual
1			Leads			Leads			
2			Follow-up			Follow-up			
Total									

Consistency Rate: Total Actual (A)/Budget (B)									

Friday: _____

	Budgeted Time		Growth Factors	Actual Time				Time In Minutes	
	Start	End	Budgeted Activity	Start	End	Actual Activity		Budget	Actual
1	10:00am	11:00 am	Leads	10:00am	11:00 am	Leads			
2	11:00am	11:30 am	Follow-up	11:00am	11:20 am	Follow-up			
Total									

Consistency Rate: Total Actual (A)/Budget (B)									

Conversion Rate Scoreboard

Growth Factor	Monday	Tuesday	Wednesday	Thursday	Friday	Week 2
Leads (L)						
Members (M)						
Conversion Rate: M/L						

Quarterly Scoreboard

Pull from week 2 above. The average from Monday to Friday

Growth Factors	W1	W2	W3	W4	W5	W6	W7	W8	W9	W10	W11	W12	W13	Ave/ Tot
Consistency %														
Leads														
Members														
Conversion %														

Consistency Rate Scoreboard – Week 3

Monday: _____

	Budgeted Time		Growth Factors	Actual Time			Time In Minutes	
	Start	End	Budgeted Activity	Start	End	Actual Activity	Budget	Actual
1			Leads			Leads		
2			Follow-up			Follow-up		
Total								

Consistency Rate: Total Actual (A)/Budget (B)

Tuesday: _____

	Budgeted Time		Growth Factors	Actual Time			Time In Minutes	
	Start	End	Budgeted Activity	Start	End	Actual Activity	Budget	Actual
1			Leads			Leads		
2			Follow-up			Follow-up		
Total								

Consistency Rate: Total Actual (A)/Budget (B)

Wednesday: _____

	Budgeted Time		Growth Factors	Actual Time			Time In Minutes	
	Start	End	Budgeted Activity	Start	End	Actual Activity	Budget	Actual
1			Leads			Leads		
2			Follow-up			Follow-up		
Total								

Consistency Rate: Total Actual (A)/Budget (B)

Thursday: _____

	Budgeted Time		Growth Factors	Actual Time			Time In Minutes	
	Start	End	Budgeted Activity	Start	End	Actual Activity	Budget	Actual
1			Leads			Leads		
2			Follow-up			Follow-up		
Total								

	Consistency Rate: Total Actual (A)/Budget (B)						
Friday: _____							
	Budgeted Time		**Growth Factors**	**Actual Time**			**Time In Minutes**	
	Start	End	Budgeted Activity	Start	End	Actual Activity	Budget	Actual
1	10:00am	11:00 am	Leads	10:00am	11:00 am	Leads		
2	11:00am	11:30 am	Follow-up	11:00am	11:20 am	Follow-up		
Total								
Consistency Rate: Total Actual (A)/Budget (B)								

Consistency Rate Scoreboard

Growth Factor	**Monday**	**Tuesday**	**Wednesday**	**Thursday**	**Friday**	**Week 3**
Leads (L)						
Members (M)						
Conversion Rate: M/L						

Quarterly Scoreboard

Pull from week 3 above. The average from Monday to Friday

Growth Factors	**W1**	**W2**	**W3**	**W4**	**W5**	**W6**	**W7**	**W8**	**W9**	**W10**	**W11**	**W12**	**W13**	**Ave/Tot**
Consistency %														
Leads														
Members														
Conversion %														

Consistency Rate Scoreboard – Week 4

Monday: _____							
	Budgeted Time		**Growth Factors**	**Actual Time**			**Time In Minutes**	
	Start	End	Budgeted Activity	Start	End	Actual Activity	Budget	Actual
1			Leads			Leads		
2			Follow-up			Follow-up		
Total								
Consistency Rate: Total Actual (A)/Budget (B)								
Tuesday: _____								
	Budgeted Time		**Growth Factors**	**Actual Time**			**Time In Minutes**	
	Start	End	Budgeted Activity	Start	End	Actual Activity	Budget	Actual

1			Leads			Leads			
2			Follow-up			Follow-up			
Total									
Consistency Rate: Total Actual (A)/Budget (B)									

Wednesday: _____

	Budgeted Time		Growth Factors	Actual Time			Time In Minutes	
	Start	End	Budgeted Activity	Start	End	Actual Activity	Budget	Actual
1			Leads			Leads		
2			Follow-up			Follow-up		
Total								
Consistency Rate: Total Actual (A)/Budget (B)								

Thursday: _____

	Budgeted Time		Growth Factors	Actual Time			Time In Minutes	
	Start	End	Budgeted Activity	Start	End	Actual Activity	Budget	Actual
1			Leads			Leads		
2			Follow-up			Follow-up		
Total								
Consistency Rate: Total Actual (A)/Budget (B)								

Friday: _____

	Budgeted Time		Growth Factors	Actual Time			Time In Minutes	
	Start	End	Budgeted Activity	Start	End	Actual Activity	Budget	Actual
1	10:00am	11:00 am	Leads	10:00am	11:00 am	Leads		
2	11:00am	11:30 am	Follow-up	11:00am	11:20 am	Follow-up		
Total								
Consistency Rate: Total Actual (A)/Budget (B)								

Consistency Rate Scoreboard

Growth Factor	Monday	Tuesday	Wednesday	Thursday	Friday	Week 3
Leads (L)						
Members (M)						
Conversion Rate: M/L						

Quarterly Scoreboard

Pull from week 4 above. The average from Monday to Friday

Growth Factors	W1	W2	W3	W4	W5	W6	W7	W8	W9	W10	W11	W12	W13	Ave/ Tot
Consistency %														
Leads														
Members														
Conversion %														

Consistency Rate Scoreboard – Week 5

Monday: _____

	Budgeted Time		Growth Factors	Actual Time			Time In Minutes	
	Start	End	Budgeted Activity	Start	End	Actual Activity	Budget	Actual
1			Leads			Leads		
2			Follow-up			Follow-up		
Total								

Consistency Rate: Total Actual (A)/Budget (B)

Tuesday: _____

	Budgeted Time		Growth Factors	Actual Time			Time In Minutes	
	Start	End	Budgeted Activity	Start	End	Actual Activity	Budget	Actual
1			Leads			Leads		
2			Follow-up			Follow-up		
Total								

Consistency Rate: Total Actual (A)/Budget (B)

Wednesday: _____

	Budgeted Time		Growth Factors	Actual Time			Time In Minutes	
	Start	End	Budgeted Activity	Start	End	Actual Activity	Budget	Actual
1			Leads			Leads		
2			Follow-up			Follow-up		
Total								

Consistency Rate: Total Actual (A)/Budget (B)

Thursday: _____

	Budgeted Time		Growth Factors	Actual Time			Time In Minutes	
	Start	End	Budgeted Activity	Start	End	Actual Activity	Budget	Actual
1			Leads			Leads		
2			Follow-up			Follow-up		
Total								

Consistency Rate: Total Actual (A)/Budget (B)								

Friday: _____

	Budgeted Time		Growth Factors	Actual Time			Time In Minutes	
	Start	End	Budgeted Activity	Start	End	Actual Activity	Budget	Actual
1	10:00am	11:00 am	Leads	10:00am	11:00 am	Leads		
2	11:00am	11:30 am	Follow-up	11:00am	11:20 am	Follow-up		
Total								
Consistency Rate: Total Actual (A)/Budget (B)								

Conversion Rate Scoreboard

Growth Factor	Monday	Tuesday	Wednesday	Thursday	Friday	Week 3
Leads (L)						
Members (M)						
Conversion Rate: M/L						

Quarterly Scoreboard

Pull from week 5 above. The average from Monday to Friday

Growth Factors	W1	W2	W3	W4	W5	W6	W7	W8	W9	W10	W11	W12	W13	Ave/Tot
Consistency %														
Leads														
Members														
Conversion %														

Consistency Rate Scoreboard – Week 6

Monday: _____

	Budgeted Time		Growth Factors	Actual Time			Time In Minutes	
	Start	End	Budgeted Activity	Start	End	Actual Activity	Budget	Actual
1			Leads			Leads		
2			Follow-up			Follow-up		
Total								

Consistency Rate: Total Actual (A)/Budget (B)								

Tuesday: _____

	Budgeted Time		Growth Factors	Actual Time			Time In Minutes	
	Start	End	Budgeted Activity	Start	End	Actual Activity	Budget	Actual
1			Leads			Leads		
2			Follow-up			Follow-up		
Total								

Consistency Rate: Total Actual (A)/Budget (B)							
Wednesday: _____							
	Budgeted Time		Growth Factors	Actual Time			Time In Minutes	
	Start	End	Budgeted Activity	Start	End	Actual Activity	Budget	Actual
1			Leads			Leads		
2			Follow-up			Follow-up		
Total								
Consistency Rate: Total Actual (A)/Budget (B)								
Thursday: _____								
	Budgeted Time		Growth Factors	Actual Time			Time In Minutes	
	Start	End	Budgeted Activity	Start	End	Actual Activity	Budget	Actual
1			Leads			Leads		
2			Follow-up			Follow-up		
Total								
Consistency Rate: Total Actual (A)/Budget (B)								
Friday: _____								
	Budgeted Time		Growth Factors	Actual Time			Time In Minutes	
	Start	End	Budgeted Activity	Start	End	Actual Activity	Budget	Actual
1	10:00am	11:00 am	Leads	10:00am	11:00 am	Leads		
2	11:00am	11:30 am	Follow-up	11:00am	11:20 am	Follow-up		
Total								
Consistency Rate: Total Actual (A)/Budget (B)								

Conversion Rate Scoreboard

Growth Factor	Monday	Tuesday	Wednesday	Thursday	Friday	Week 3
Leads (L)						
Members (M)						
Conversion Rate: M/L						

Quarterly Scoreboard

Pull from week 6 above. The average from Monday to Friday

Growth Factors	W1	W2	W3	W4	W5	W6	W7	W8	W9	W10	W11	W12	W13	Ave/Tot
Consistency %														
Leads														
Members														
Conversion %														

Consistency Rate Scoreboard – Week 7

Monday: _____

	Budgeted Time		Growth Factors	Actual Time			Time In Minutes	
	Start	End	Budgeted Activity	Start	End	Actual Activity	Budget	Actual
1			Leads			Leads		
2			Follow-up			Follow-up		
Total								

Consistency Rate: Total Actual (A)/Budget (B)

Tuesday: _____

	Budgeted Time		Growth Factors	Actual Time			Time In Minutes	
	Start	End	Budgeted Activity	Start	End	Actual Activity	Budget	Actual
1			Leads			Leads		
2			Follow-up			Follow-up		
Total								

Consistency Rate: Total Actual (A)/Budget (B)

Wednesday: _____

	Budgeted Time		Growth Factors	Actual Time			Time In Minutes	
	Start	End	Budgeted Activity	Start	End	Actual Activity	Budget	Actual
1			Leads			Leads		
2			Follow-up			Follow-up		
Total								

Consistency Rate: Total Actual (A)/Budget (B)

Thursday: _____

	Budgeted Time		Growth Factors	Actual Time			Time In Minutes	
	Start	End	Budgeted Activity	Start	End	Actual Activity	Budget	Actual
1			Leads			Leads		
2			Follow-up			Follow-up		
Total								

Consistency Rate: Total Actual (A)/Budget (B)

Friday: _____

	Budgeted Time		Growth Factors	Actual Time			Time In Minutes	
	Start	End	Budgeted Activity	Start	End	Actual Activity	Budget	Actual
1	10:00am	11:00 am	Leads	10:00am	11:00 am	Leads		
2	11:00am	11:30 am	Follow-up	11:00am	11:20 am	Follow-up		
Total								

Consistency Rate: Total Actual (A)/Budget (B)

Conversion Rate Scoreboard

Growth Factor	Monday	Tuesday	Wednesday	Thursday	Friday	Week 3
Leads (L)						
Members (M)						
Conversion Rate: M/L						

Quarterly Scoreboard

Pull from week 7 above. The average from Monday to Friday

Growth Factors	W1	W2	W3	W4	W5	W6	W7	W8	W9	W10	W11	W12	W13	Ave/Tot
Consistency %														
Leads														
Members														
Conversion %														

Consistency Rate Scoreboard – Week 8

Monday: _____

	Budgeted Time		Growth Factors	Actual Time			Time In Minutes	
	Start	End	Budgeted Activity	Start	End	Actual Activity	Budget	Actual
1			Leads			Leads		
2			Follow-up			Follow-up		
Total								
Consistency Rate: Total Actual (A)/Budget (B)								

Tuesday: _____

	Budgeted Time		Growth Factors	Actual Time			Time In Minutes	
	Start	End	Budgeted Activity	Start	End	Actual Activity	Budget	Actual
1			Leads			Leads		
2			Follow-up			Follow-up		
Total								
Consistency Rate: Total Actual (A)/Budget (B)								

Wednesday: _____

	Budgeted Time		Growth Factors	Actual Time			Time In Minutes	
	Start	End	Budgeted Activity	Start	End	Actual Activity	Budget	Actual
1			Leads			Leads		
2			Follow-up			Follow-up		
Total								
Consistency Rate: Total Actual (A)/Budget (B)								

Thursday: _____								
	Budgeted Time		Growth Factors	Actual Time			Time In Minutes	
	Start	End	Budgeted Activity	Start	End	Actual Activity	Budget	Actual
1			Leads			Leads		
2			Follow-up			Follow-up		
Total								
Consistency Rate: Total Actual (A)/Budget (B)								

Friday: _____								
	Budgeted Time		Growth Factors	Actual Time			Time In Minutes	
	Start	End	Budgeted Activity	Start	End	Actual Activity	Budget	Actual
1	10:00am	11:00 am	Leads	10:00am	11:00 am	Leads		
2	11:00am	11:30 am	Follow-up	11:00am	11:20 am	Follow-up		
Total								
Consistency Rate: Total Actual (A)/Budget (B)								

Conversion Rate Scoreboard

Growth Factor	Monday	Tuesday	Wednesday	Thursday	Friday	Week 3
Leads (L)						
Members (M)						
Conversion Rate: M/L						

Quarterly Scoreboard

Pull from week 8 above. The average from Monday to Friday

Growth Factors	W1	W2	W3	W4	W5	W6	W7	W8	W9	W10	W11	W12	W13	Ave/Tot
Consistency %														
Leads														
Members														
Conversion %														

Consistency Rate Scoreboard – Week 9

Monday: _____								
	Budgeted Time		Growth Factors	Actual Time			Time In Minutes	
	Start	End	Budgeted Activity	Start	End	Actual Activity	Budget	Actual
1			Leads			Leads		
2			Follow-up			Follow-up		
Total								

Consistency Rate: Total Actual (A)/Budget (B)							

Tuesday: _____

	Budgeted Time		Growth Factors	Actual Time			Time In Minutes	
	Start	End	Budgeted Activity	Start	End	Actual Activity	Budget	Actual
1			Leads			Leads		
2			Follow-up			Follow-up		
Total								

Consistency Rate: Total Actual (A)/Budget (B)							

Wednesday: _____

	Budgeted Time		Growth Factors	Actual Time			Time In Minutes	
	Start	End	Budgeted Activity	Start	End	Actual Activity	Budget	Actual
1			Leads			Leads		
2			Follow-up			Follow-up		
Total								

Consistency Rate: Total Actual (A)/Budget (B)							

Thursday: _____

	Budgeted Time		Growth Factors	Actual Time			Time In Minutes	
	Start	End	Budgeted Activity	Start	End	Actual Activity	Budget	Actual
1			Leads			Leads		
2			Follow-up			Follow-up		
Total								

Consistency Rate: Total Actual (A)/Budget (B)							

Friday: _____

	Budgeted Time		Growth Factors	Actual Time			Time In Minutes	
	Start	End	Budgeted Activity	Start	End	Actual Activity	Budget	Actual
1	10:00am	11:00 am	Leads	10:00am	11:00 am	Leads		
2	11:00am	11:30 am	Follow-up	11:00am	11:20 am	Follow-up		
Total								

Consistency Rate: Total Actual (A)/Budget (B)							

Conversion Rate Scoreboard

Growth Factor	Monday	Tuesday	Wednesday	Thursday	Friday	Week 3
Leads (L)						
Members (M)						
Conversion Rate: M/L						

Quarterly Scoreboard

Pull from week 9 above. The average from Monday to Friday

Growth Factors	W1	W2	W3	W4	W5	W6	W7	W8	W9	W10	W11	W12	W13	Ave/ Tot
Consistency %														
Leads														
Members														
Conversion %														

Consistency Rate Scoreboard – Week 10

Monday: _____

	Budgeted Time		Growth Factors	Actual Time			Time In Minutes	
	Start	End	Budgeted Activity	Start	End	Actual Activity	Budget	Actual
1			Leads			Leads		
2			Follow-up			Follow-up		
Total								

Consistency Rate: Total Actual (A)/Budget (B)

Tuesday: _____

	Budgeted Time		Growth Factors	Actual Time			Time In Minutes	
	Start	End	Budgeted Activity	Start	End	Actual Activity	Budget	Actual
1			Leads			Leads		
2			Follow-up			Follow-up		
Total								

Consistency Rate: Total Actual (A)/Budget (B)

Wednesday: _____

	Budgeted Time		Growth Factors	Actual Time			Time In Minutes	
	Start	End	Budgeted Activity	Start	End	Actual Activity	Budget	Actual
1			Leads			Leads		
2			Follow-up			Follow-up		
Total								

Consistency Rate: Total Actual (A)/Budget (B)

Thursday: _____

	Budgeted Time		Growth Factors	Actual Time			Time In Minutes	
	Start	End	Budgeted Activity	Start	End	Actual Activity	Budget	Actual
1			Leads			Leads		
2			Follow-up			Follow-up		
Total								

	Consistency Rate: Total Actual (A)/Budget (B)							

Friday: _____

	Budgeted Time		Growth Factors	Actual Time			Time In Minutes	
	Start	End	Budgeted Activity	Start	End	Actual Activity	Budget	Actual
1	10:00am	11:00 am	Leads	10:00am	11:00 am	Leads		
2	11:00am	11:30 am	Follow-up	11:00am	11:20 am	Follow-up		
Total								
Consistency Rate: Total Actual (A)/Budget (B)								

Conversion Rate Scoreboard

Growth Factor	Monday	Tuesday	Wednesday	Thursday	Friday	Week 3
Leads (L)						
Members (M)						
Conversion Rate: M/L						

Quarterly Scoreboard

Pull from week 10 above. The average from Monday to Friday

Growth Factors	W1	W2	W3	W4	W5	W6	W7	W8	W9	W10	W11	W12	W13	Ave/Tot
Consistency %														
Leads														
Members														
Conversion %														

Consistency Rate Scoreboard – Week 11

Monday: _____

	Budgeted Time		Growth Factors	Actual Time			Time In Minutes	
	Start	End	Budgeted Activity	Start	End	Actual Activity	Budget	Actual
1			Leads			Leads		
2			Follow-up			Follow-up		
Total								
Consistency Rate: Total Actual (A)/Budget (B)								

Tuesday: _____

	Budgeted Time		Growth Factors	Actual Time			Time In Minutes	
	Start	End	Budgeted Activity	Start	End	Actual Activity	Budget	Actual

1			Leads			Leads	
2			Follow-up			Follow-up	
Total							
Consistency Rate: Total Actual (A)/Budget (B)							

Wednesday: _____

	Budgeted Time		Growth Factors	Actual Time			Time In Minutes	
	Start	End	Budgeted Activity	Start	End	Actual Activity	Budget	Actual
1			Leads			Leads		
2			Follow-up			Follow-up		
Total								
Consistency Rate: Total Actual (A)/Budget (B)								

Thursday: _____

	Budgeted Time		Growth Factors	Actual Time			Time In Minutes	
	Start	End	Budgeted Activity	Start	End	Actual Activity	Budget	Actual
1			Leads			Leads		
2			Follow-up			Follow-up		
Total								
Consistency Rate: Total Actual (A)/Budget (B)								

Friday: _____

	Budgeted Time		Growth Factors	Actual Time			Time In Minutes	
	Start	End	Budgeted Activity	Start	End	Actual Activity	Budget	Actual
1	10:00am	11:00 am	Leads	10:00am	11:00 am	Leads		
2	11:00am	11:30 am	Follow-up	11:00am	11:20 am	Follow-up		
Total								
Consistency Rate: Total Actual (A)/Budget (B)								

Conversion Rate Scoreboard

Growth Factor	Monday	Tuesday	Wednesday	Thursday	Friday	Week 3
Leads (L)						
Members (M)						
Conversion Rate: M/L						

Quarterly Scoreboard

Pull from week 11 above. The average from Monday to Friday

Growth Factors	W1	W2	W3	W4	W5	W6	W7	W8	W9	W10	W11	W12	W13	Ave/Tot
Consistency %														
Leads														
Members														
Conversion %														

Consistency Rate Scoreboard – Week 12

Monday: _____

	Budgeted Time		Growth Factors	Actual Time			Time In Minutes	
	Start	End	Budgeted Activity	Start	End	Actual Activity	Budget	Actual
1			Leads			Leads		
2			Follow-up			Follow-up		
Total								

Consistency Rate: Total Actual (A)/Budget (B)

Tuesday: _____

	Budgeted Time		Growth Factors	Actual Time			Time In Minutes	
	Start	End	Budgeted Activity	Start	End	Actual Activity	Budget	Actual
1			Leads			Leads		
2			Follow-up			Follow-up		
Total								

Consistency Rate: Total Actual (A)/Budget (B)

Wednesday: _____

	Budgeted Time		Growth Factors	Actual Time			Time In Minutes	
	Start	End	Budgeted Activity	Start	End	Actual Activity	Budget	Actual
1			Leads			Leads		
2			Follow-up			Follow-up		
Total								

Consistency Rate: Total Actual (A)/Budget (B)

Thursday: _____

	Budgeted Time		Growth Factors	Actual Time			Time In Minutes	
	Start	End	Budgeted Activity	Start	End	Actual Activity	Budget	Actual
1			Leads			Leads		
2			Follow-up			Follow-up		
Total								

	Consistency Rate: Total Actual (A)/Budget (B)							

Friday: _____

	Budgeted Time		Growth Factors	Actual Time			Time In Minutes	
	Start	End	Budgeted Activity	Start	End	Actual Activity	Budget	Actual
1	10:00am	11:00 am	Leads	10:00am	11:00 am	Leads		
2	11:00am	11:30 am	Follow-up	11:00am	11:20 am	Follow-up		
Total								
Consistency Rate: Total Actual (A)/Budget (B)								

Conversion Rate Scoreboard

Growth Factor	Monday	Tuesday	Wednesday	Thursday	Friday	Week 3
Leads (L)						
Members (M)						
Conversion Rate: M/L						

Quarterly Scoreboard

Pull from week 12 above. The average from Monday to Friday

Growth Factors	W1	W2	W3	W4	W5	W6	W7	W8	W9	W10	W11	W12	W13	Ave/ Tot
Consistency %														
Leads														
Members														
Conversion %														

Consistency Rate Scoreboard – Week 13

	Monday: _____							

	Budgeted Time		Growth Factors	Actual Time			Time In Minutes	
	Start	End	Budgeted Activity	Start	End	Actual Activity	Budget	Actual
1			Leads			Leads		
2			Follow-up			Follow-up		
Total								

Consistency Rate: Total Actual (A)/Budget (B)									
Tuesday: _____									
	Budgeted Time		Growth Factors	Actual Time				Time In Minutes	
	Start	End	Budgeted Activity	Start	End	Actual Activity		Budget	Actual
1			Leads			Leads			
2			Follow-up			Follow-up			
Total									
Consistency Rate: Total Actual (A)/Budget (B)									
Wednesday: _____									
	Budgeted Time		Growth Factors	Actual Time				Time In Minutes	
	Start	End	Budgeted Activity	Start	End	Actual Activity		Budget	Actual
1			Leads			Leads			
2			Follow-up			Follow-up			
Total									
Consistency Rate: Total Actual (A)/Budget (B)									
Thursday: _____									
	Budgeted Time		Growth Factors	Actual Time				Time In Minutes	
	Start	End	Budgeted Activity	Start	End	Actual Activity		Budget	Actual
1			Leads			Leads			
2			Follow-up			Follow-up			
Total									
Consistency Rate: Total Actual (A)/Budget (B)									
Friday: _____									
	Budgeted Time		Growth Factors	Actual Time				Time In Minutes	
	Start	End	Budgeted Activity	Start	End	Actual Activity		Budget	Actual
1	10:00am	11:00 am	Leads	10:00am	11:00 am	Leads			
2	11:00am	11:30 am	Follow-up	11:00am	11:20 am	Follow-up			
Total									
Consistency Rate: Total Actual (A)/Budget (B)									

Conversion Rate Scoreboard

Growth Factor	Monday	Tuesday	Wednesday	Thursday	Friday	Week 3
Leads (L)						
Members (M)						
Conversion Rate: M/L						

Quarterly Scoreboard

Pull from week 13 above. The average from Monday to Friday

Growth Factors	W1	W2	W3	W4	W5	W6	W7	W8	W9	W10	W11	W12	W13	Ave/Tot
Consistency %														
Leads														
Members														
Conversion %														

Q2 Accountability Scoreboard Templates

Consistency Rate Scoreboard – Week 1

Monday: _____

	Budgeted Time		Growth Factors	Actual Time			Time In Minutes	
	Start	End	Budgeted Activity	Start	End	Actual Activity	Budget	Actual
1			Leads			Leads		
2			Follow-up			Follow-up		
Total								

Consistency Rate: Total Actual (A)/Budget (B)

Tuesday: _____

	Budgeted Time		Growth Factors	Actual Time			Time In Minutes	
	Start	End	Budgeted Activity	Start	End	Actual Activity	Budget	Actual
1			Leads			Leads		
2			Follow-up			Follow-up		
Total								

Consistency Rate: Total Actual (A)/Budget (B)

Wednesday: _____

	Budgeted Time		Growth Factors	Actual Time			Time In Minutes	
	Start	End	Budgeted Activity	Start	End	Actual Activity	Budget	Actual
1			Leads			Leads		
2			Follow-up			Follow-up		
Total								

Consistency Rate: Total Actual (A)/Budget (B)

Thursday: _____

	Budgeted Time		Growth Factors	Actual Time			Time In Minutes	
	Start	End	Budgeted Activity	Start	End	Actual Activity	Budget	Actual
1			Leads			Leads		
2			Follow-up			Follow-up		
Total								

Consistency Rate: Total Actual (A)/Budget (B)								

Friday: _____

	Budgeted Time		Growth Factors	Actual Time			Time In Minutes	
	Start	End	Budgeted Activity	Start	End	Actual Activity	Budget	Actual
1	10:00am	11:00 am	Leads	10:00am	11:00 am	Leads		
2	11:00am	11:30 am	Follow-up	11:00am	11:20 am	Follow-up		
Total								
Consistency Rate: Total Actual (A)/Budget (B)								

Conversion Rate Scoreboard

Growth Factor	Monday	Tuesday	Wednesday	Thursday	Friday	Week 3
Leads (L)						
Members (M)						
Conversion Rate: M/L						

Quarterly Scoreboard

Pull from week 1 above. The average from Monday to Friday

Growth Factors	W1	W2	W3	W4	W5	W6	W7	W8	W9	W10	W11	W12	W13	Ave/Tot
Consistency %														
Leads														
Members														
Conversion %														

Consistency Rate Scoreboard – Week 2

Monday: _____								
	Budgeted Time		Growth Factors	Actual Time			Time In Minutes	
	Start	End	Budgeted Activity	Start	End	Actual Activity	Budget	Actual
1			Leads			Leads		
2			Follow-up			Follow-up		
Total								
Consistency Rate: Total Actual (A)/Budget (B)								

Tuesday: _____

	Budgeted Time		Growth Factors	Actual Time			Time In Minutes	
	Start	End	Budgeted Activity	Start	End	Actual Activity	Budget	Actual
1			Leads			Leads		
2			Follow-up			Follow-up		
Total								
Consistency Rate: Total Actual (A)/Budget (B)								

Wednesday: _____

	Budgeted Time		Growth Factors	Actual Time			Time In Minutes	
	Start	End	Budgeted Activity	Start	End	Actual Activity	Budget	Actual
1			Leads			Leads		
2			Follow-up			Follow-up		
Total								
Consistency Rate: Total Actual (A)/Budget (B)								

Thursday: _____

	Budgeted Time		Growth Factors	Actual Time			Time In Minutes	
	Start	End	Budgeted Activity	Start	End	Actual Activity	Budget	Actual
1			Leads			Leads		
2			Follow-up			Follow-up		
Total								
Consistency Rate: Total Actual (A)/Budget (B)								

Friday: _____

	Budgeted Time		Growth Factors	Actual Time			Time In Minutes	
	Start	End	Budgeted Activity	Start	End	Actual Activity	Budget	Actual
1	10:00am	11:00 am	Leads	10:00am	11:00 am	Leads		
2	11:00am	11:30 am	Follow-up	11:00am	11:20 am	Follow-up		
Total								
Consistency Rate: Total Actual (A)/Budget (B)								

Conversion Rate Scoreboard

Growth Factor	Monday	Tuesday	Wednesday	Thursday	Friday	Week 3
Leads (L)						
Members (M)						
Conversion Rate: M/L						

Quarterly Scoreboard

Pull from week 2 above. The average from Monday to Friday

Growth Factors	W1	W2	W3	W4	W5	W6	W7	W8	W9	W10	W11	W12	W13	Ave/ Tot
Consistency %														
Leads														
Members														
Conversion %														

Consistency Rate Scoreboard – Week 3

Monday: _____

	Budgeted Time		Growth Factors	Actual Time			Time In Minutes	
	Start	End	Budgeted Activity	Start	End	Actual Activity	Budget	Actual
1			Leads			Leads		
2			Follow-up			Follow-up		
Total								

Consistency Rate: Total Actual (A)/Budget (B)

Tuesday: _____

	Budgeted Time		Growth Factors	Actual Time			Time In Minutes	
	Start	End	Budgeted Activity	Start	End	Actual Activity	Budget	Actual
1			Leads			Leads		
2			Follow-up			Follow-up		
Total								

Consistency Rate: Total Actual (A)/Budget (B)

Wednesday: _____

	Budgeted Time		Growth Factors	Actual Time			Time In Minutes	
	Start	End	Budgeted Activity	Start	End	Actual Activity	Budget	Actual
1			Leads			Leads		
2			Follow-up			Follow-up		
Total								

Consistency Rate: Total Actual (A)/Budget (B)

Thursday: _____

	Budgeted Time		Growth Factors	Actual Time			Time In Minutes	
	Start	End	Budgeted Activity	Start	End	Actual Activity	Budget	Actual
1			Leads			Leads		
2			Follow-up			Follow-up		
Total								

	Consistency Rate: Total Actual (A)/Budget (B)							
Friday: _____								
	Budgeted Time		Growth Factors	Actual Time			Time In Minutes	
	Start	End	Budgeted Activity	Start	End	Actual Activity	Budget	Actual
1	10:00am	11:00 am	Leads	10:00am	11:00 am	Leads		
2	11:00am	11:30 am	Follow-up	11:00am	11:20 am	Follow-up		
Total								
Consistency Rate: Total Actual (A)/Budget (B)								

Conversion Rate Scoreboard

Growth Factor	Monday	Tuesday	Wednesday	Thursday	Friday	Week 3
Leads (L)						
Members (M)						
Conversion Rate: M/L						

Quarterly Scoreboard

Pull from week 3 above. The average from Monday to Friday

Growth Factors	W1	W2	W3	W4	W5	W6	W7	W8	W9	W10	W11	W12	W13	Ave/Tot
Consistency %														
Leads														
Members														
Conversion %														

Consistency Rate Scoreboard – Week 4

	Monday: _____							
	Budgeted Time		Growth Factors	Actual Time			Time In Minutes	
	Start	End	Budgeted Activity	Start	End	Actual Activity	Budget	Actual
1			Leads			Leads		
2			Follow-up			Follow-up		
Total								
Consistency Rate: Total Actual (A)/Budget (B)								

Tuesday: _____

	Budgeted Time		Growth Factors	Actual Time			Time In Minutes	
	Start	End	Budgeted Activity	Start	End	Actual Activity	Budget	Actual
1			Leads			Leads		
2			Follow-up			Follow-up		
Total								
Consistency Rate: Total Actual (A)/Budget (B)								

Wednesday: _____

	Budgeted Time		Growth Factors	Actual Time			Time In Minutes	
	Start	End	Budgeted Activity	Start	End	Actual Activity	Budget	Actual
1			Leads			Leads		
2			Follow-up			Follow-up		
Total								
Consistency Rate: Total Actual (A)/Budget (B)								

Thursday: _____

	Budgeted Time		Growth Factors	Actual Time			Time In Minutes	
	Start	End	Budgeted Activity	Start	End	Actual Activity	Budget	Actual
1			Leads			Leads		
2			Follow-up			Follow-up		
Total								
Consistency Rate: Total Actual (A)/Budget (B)								

Friday: _____

	Budgeted Time		Growth Factors	Actual Time			Time In Minutes	
	Start	End	Budgeted Activity	Start	End	Actual Activity	Budget	Actual
1	10:00am	11:00 am	Leads	10:00am	11:00 am	Leads		
2	11:00am	11:30 am	Follow-up	11:00am	11:20 am	Follow-up		
Total								
Consistency Rate: Total Actual (A)/Budget (B)								

Conversion Rate Scoreboard

Growth Factor	Monday	Tuesday	Wednesday	Thursday	Friday	Week 3
Leads (L)						
Members (M)						
Conversion Rate: M/L						

Quarterly Scoreboard

Pull from week 4 above. The average from Monday to Friday

Growth Factors	W1	W2	W3	W4	W5	W6	W7	W8	W9	W10	W11	W12	W13	Ave/ Tot
Consistency %														
Leads														
Members														
Conversion %														

Consistency Rate Scoreboard – Week 5

Monday: _____

	Budgeted Time		Growth Factors	Actual Time			Time In Minutes	
	Start	End	Budgeted Activity	Start	End	Actual Activity	Budget	Actual
1			Leads			Leads		
2			Follow-up			Follow-up		
Total								

Consistency Rate: Total Actual (A)/Budget (B)

Tuesday: _____

	Budgeted Time		Growth Factors	Actual Time			Time In Minutes	
	Start	End	Budgeted Activity	Start	End	Actual Activity	Budget	Actual
1			Leads			Leads		
2			Follow-up			Follow-up		
Total								

Consistency Rate: Total Actual (A)/Budget (B)

Wednesday: _____

	Budgeted Time		Growth Factors	Actual Time			Time In Minutes	
	Start	End	Budgeted Activity	Start	End	Actual Activity	Budget	Actual
1			Leads			Leads		
2			Follow-up			Follow-up		
Total								

Consistency Rate: Total Actual (A)/Budget (B)

Thursday: _____

	Budgeted Time		Growth Factors	Actual Time			Time In Minutes	
	Start	End	Budgeted Activity	Start	End	Actual Activity	Budget	Actual
1			Leads			Leads		
2			Follow-up			Follow-up		
Total								

	Consistency Rate: Total Actual (A)/Budget (B)						

Friday: _____

	Budgeted Time		Growth Factors	Actual Time			Time In Minutes	
	Start	End	Budgeted Activity	Start	End	Actual Activity	Budget	Actual
1	10:00am	11:00 am	Leads	10:00am	11:00 am	Leads		
2	11:00am	11:30 am	Follow-up	11:00am	11:20 am	Follow-up		
Total								
Consistency Rate: Total Actual (A)/Budget (B)								

Conversion Rate Scoreboard

Growth Factor	Monday	Tuesday	Wednesday	Thursday	Friday	Week 3
Leads (L)						
Members (M)						
Conversion Rate: M/L						

Quarterly Scoreboard

Pull from week 5 above. The average from Monday to Friday

Growth Factors	W1	W2	W3	W4	W5	W6	W7	W8	W9	W10	W11	W12	W13	Ave/Tot
Consistency %														
Leads														
Members														
Conversion %														

Consistency Rate Scoreboard – Week 6

Monday: _____

	Budgeted Time		Growth Factors	Actual Time			Time In Minutes	
	Start	End	Budgeted Activity	Start	End	Actual Activity	Budget	Actual
1			Leads			Leads		
2			Follow-up			Follow-up		
Total								

Consistency Rate: Total Actual (A)/Budget (B)							

Tuesday: _____

	Budgeted Time		Growth Factors	Actual Time			Time In Minutes	
	Start	End	Budgeted Activity	Start	End	Actual Activity	Budget	Actual
1			Leads			Leads		
2			Follow-up			Follow-up		
Total								

Consistency Rate: Total Actual (A)/Budget (B)							

Wednesday: _____

	Budgeted Time		Growth Factors	Actual Time			Time In Minutes	
	Start	End	Budgeted Activity	Start	End	Actual Activity	Budget	Actual
1			Leads			Leads		
2			Follow-up			Follow-up		
Total								

Consistency Rate: Total Actual (A)/Budget (B)							

Thursday: _____

	Budgeted Time		Growth Factors	Actual Time			Time In Minutes	
	Start	End	Budgeted Activity	Start	End	Actual Activity	Budget	Actual
1			Leads			Leads		
2			Follow-up			Follow-up		
Total								

Consistency Rate: Total Actual (A)/Budget (B)							

Friday: _____

	Budgeted Time		Growth Factors	Actual Time			Time In Minutes	
	Start	End	Budgeted Activity	Start	End	Actual Activity	Budget	Actual
1	10:00am	11:00 am	Leads	10:00am	11:00 am	Leads		
2	11:00am	11:30 am	Follow-up	11:00am	11:20 am	Follow-up		
Total								

Consistency Rate: Total Actual (A)/Budget (B)							

Conversion Rate Scoreboard

Growth Factor	Monday	Tuesday	Wednesday	Thursday	Friday	Week 3
Leads (L)						
Members (M)						
Conversion Rate: M/L						

Quarterly Scoreboard

Pull from week 6 above. The average from Monday to Friday

Growth Factors	W1	W2	W3	W4	W5	W6	W7	W8	W9	W10	W11	W12	W13	Ave/ Tot
Consistency %														
Leads														
Members														
Conversion %														

Consistency Rate Scoreboard – Week 7

Monday: _____

	Budgeted Time		Growth Factors	Actual Time			Time In Minutes	
	Start	End	Budgeted Activity	Start	End	Actual Activity	Budget	Actual
1			Leads			Leads		
2			Follow-up			Follow-up		
Total								

Consistency Rate: Total Actual (A)/Budget (B)

Tuesday: _____

	Budgeted Time		Growth Factors	Actual Time			Time In Minutes	
	Start	End	Budgeted Activity	Start	End	Actual Activity	Budget	Actual
1			Leads			Leads		
2			Follow-up			Follow-up		
Total								

Consistency Rate: Total Actual (A)/Budget (B)

Wednesday: _____

	Budgeted Time		Growth Factors	Actual Time			Time In Minutes	
	Start	End	Budgeted Activity	Start	End	Actual Activity	Budget	Actual
1			Leads			Leads		
2			Follow-up			Follow-up		
Total								

Consistency Rate: Total Actual (A)/Budget (B)

Thursday: _____

	Budgeted Time		Growth Factors	Actual Time			Time In Minutes	
	Start	End	Budgeted Activity	Start	End	Actual Activity	Budget	Actual
1			Leads			Leads		
2			Follow-up			Follow-up		
Total								

	Consistency Rate: Total Actual (A)/Budget (B)							

Friday: _____

	Budgeted Time		Growth Factors	Actual Time			Time In Minutes	
	Start	End	Budgeted Activity	Start	End	Actual Activity	Budget	Actual
1	10:00am	11:00 am	Leads	10:00am	11:00 am	Leads		
2	11:00am	11:30 am	Follow-up	11:00am	11:20 am	Follow-up		
Total								
Consistency Rate: Total Actual (A)/Budget (B)								

Conversion Rate Scoreboard

Growth Factor	Monday	Tuesday	Wednesday	Thursday	Friday	Week 3
Leads (L)						
Members (M)						
Conversion Rate: M/L						

Quarterly Scoreboard

Pull from week 7 above. The average from Monday to Friday

Growth Factors	W1	W2	W3	W4	W5	W6	W7	W8	W9	W10	W11	W12	W13	Ave/Tot
Consistency %														
Leads														
Members														
Conversion %														

Consistency Rate Scoreboard – Week 8

Monday: _____

	Budgeted Time		Growth Factors	Actual Time			Time In Minutes	
	Start	End	Budgeted Activity	Start	End	Actual Activity	Budget	Actual
1			Leads			Leads		
2			Follow-up			Follow-up		
Total								
Consistency Rate: Total Actual (A)/Budget (B)								

Tuesday: _____

	Budgeted Time		Growth Factors	Actual Time			Time In Minutes	
	Start	End	Budgeted Activity	Start	End	Actual Activity	Budget	Actual

	Budgeted Time		Growth Factors	Actual Time			Time In Minutes	
	Start	End	Budgeted Activity	Start	End	Actual Activity	Budget	Actual
1			Leads			Leads		
2			Follow-up			Follow-up		
Total								
Consistency Rate: Total Actual (A)/Budget (B)								

Wednesday: _____

	Budgeted Time		Growth Factors	Actual Time			Time In Minutes	
	Start	End	Budgeted Activity	Start	End	Actual Activity	Budget	Actual
1			Leads			Leads		
2			Follow-up			Follow-up		
Total								
Consistency Rate: Total Actual (A)/Budget (B)								

Thursday: _____

	Budgeted Time		Growth Factors	Actual Time			Time In Minutes	
	Start	End	Budgeted Activity	Start	End	Actual Activity	Budget	Actual
1			Leads			Leads		
2			Follow-up			Follow-up		
Total								
Consistency Rate: Total Actual (A)/Budget (B)								

Friday: _____

	Budgeted Time		Growth Factors	Actual Time			Time In Minutes	
	Start	End	Budgeted Activity	Start	End	Actual Activity	Budget	Actual
1	10:00am	11:00 am	Leads	10:00am	11:00 am	Leads		
2	11:00am	11:30 am	Follow-up	11:00am	11:20 am	Follow-up		
Total								
Consistency Rate: Total Actual (A)/Budget (B)								

Conversion Rate Scoreboard

Growth Factor	Monday	Tuesday	Wednesday	Thursday	Friday	Week 3
Leads (L)						
Members (M)						
Conversion Rate: M/L						

Quarterly Scoreboard

Pull from week 8 above. The average from Monday to Friday

Growth Factors	W1	W2	W3	W4	W5	W6	W7	W8	W9	W10	W11	W12	W13	Ave/Tot
Consistency %														
Leads														
Members														
Conversion %														

Consistency Rate Scoreboard – Week 9

Monday: _____

	Budgeted Time		Growth Factors	Actual Time			Time In Minutes	
	Start	End	Budgeted Activity	Start	End	Actual Activity	Budget	Actual
1			Leads			Leads		
2			Follow-up			Follow-up		
Total								

Consistency Rate: Total Actual (A)/Budget (B)

Tuesday: _____

	Budgeted Time		Growth Factors	Actual Time			Time In Minutes	
	Start	End	Budgeted Activity	Start	End	Actual Activity	Budget	Actual
1			Leads			Leads		
2			Follow-up			Follow-up		
Total								

Consistency Rate: Total Actual (A)/Budget (B)

Wednesday: _____

	Budgeted Time		Growth Factors	Actual Time			Time In Minutes	
	Start	End	Budgeted Activity	Start	End	Actual Activity	Budget	Actual
1			Leads			Leads		
2			Follow-up			Follow-up		
Total								

Consistency Rate: Total Actual (A)/Budget (B)

Thursday: _____

	Budgeted Time		Growth Factors	Actual Time			Time In Minutes	
	Start	End	Budgeted Activity	Start	End	Actual Activity	Budget	Actual
1			Leads			Leads		
2			Follow-up			Follow-up		
Total								

	Budgeted Time		Growth Factors	Actual Time			Time In Minutes	
Consistency Rate: Total Actual (A)/Budget (B)								
Friday: _____								
	Start	End	Budgeted Activity	Start	End	Actual Activity	Budget	Actual
1	10:00am	11:00 am	Leads	10:00am	11:00 am	Leads		
2	11:00am	11:30 am	Follow-up	11:00am	11:20 am	Follow-up		
Total								
Consistency Rate: Total Actual (A)/Budget (B)								

Conversion Rate Scoreboard

Growth Factor	Monday	Tuesday	Wednesday	Thursday	Friday	Week 3
Leads (L)						
Members (M)						
Conversion Rate: M/L						

Quarterly Scoreboard

Pull from week 9 above. The average from Monday to Friday

Growth Factors	W1	W2	W3	W4	W5	W6	W7	W8	W9	W10	W11	W12	W13	Ave/Tot
Consistency %														
Leads														
Members														
Conversion %														

Consistency Rate Scoreboard – Week 10

	Budgeted Time		Growth Factors	Actual Time			Time In Minutes	
Monday: _____								
	Start	End	Budgeted Activity	Start	End	Actual Activity	Budget	Actual
1			Leads			Leads		
2			Follow-up			Follow-up		
Total								

Consistency Rate: Total Actual (A)/Budget (B)								

Tuesday: _____

	Budgeted Time		Growth Factors	Actual Time			Time In Minutes	
	Start	End	Budgeted Activity	Start	End	Actual Activity	Budget	Actual
1			Leads			Leads		
2			Follow-up			Follow-up		
Total								

Consistency Rate: Total Actual (A)/Budget (B)								

Wednesday: _____

	Budgeted Time		Growth Factors	Actual Time			Time In Minutes	
	Start	End	Budgeted Activity	Start	End	Actual Activity	Budget	Actual
1			Leads			Leads		
2			Follow-up			Follow-up		
Total								

Consistency Rate: Total Actual (A)/Budget (B)								

Thursday: _____

	Budgeted Time		Growth Factors	Actual Time			Time In Minutes	
	Start	End	Budgeted Activity	Start	End	Actual Activity	Budget	Actual
1			Leads			Leads		
2			Follow-up			Follow-up		
Total								

Consistency Rate: Total Actual (A)/Budget (B)								

Friday: _____

	Budgeted Time		Growth Factors	Actual Time			Time In Minutes	
	Start	End	Budgeted Activity	Start	End	Actual Activity	Budget	Actual
1	10:00am	11:00 am	Leads	10:00am	11:00 am	Leads		
2	11:00am	11:30 am	Follow-up	11:00am	11:20 am	Follow-up		
Total								

Consistency Rate: Total Actual (A)/Budget (B)								

Conversion Rate Scoreboard

Growth Factor	Monday	Tuesday	Wednesday	Thursday	Friday	Week 3
Leads (L)						
Members (M)						
Conversion Rate: M/L						

Quarterly Scoreboard

Pull from week 10 above. The average from Monday to Friday

Growth Factors	W1	W2	W3	W4	W5	W6	W7	W8	W9	W10	W11	W12	W13	Ave/Tot
Consistency %														
Leads														
Members														
Conversion %														

Consistency Rate Scoreboard – Week 11

Monday: _____

	Budgeted Time		Growth Factors	Actual Time			Time In Minutes	
	Start	End	Budgeted Activity	Start	End	Actual Activity	Budget	Actual
1			Leads			Leads		
2			Follow-up			Follow-up		
Total								

Consistency Rate: Total Actual (A)/Budget (B)

Tuesday: _____

	Budgeted Time		Growth Factors	Actual Time			Time In Minutes	
	Start	End	Budgeted Activity	Start	End	Actual Activity	Budget	Actual
1			Leads			Leads		
2			Follow-up			Follow-up		
Total								

Consistency Rate: Total Actual (A)/Budget (B)

Wednesday: _____

	Budgeted Time		Growth Factors	Actual Time			Time In Minutes	
	Start	End	Budgeted Activity	Start	End	Actual Activity	Budget	Actual
1			Leads			Leads		
2			Follow-up			Follow-up		
Total								

Consistency Rate: Total Actual (A)/Budget (B)

Thursday: _____

	Budgeted Time		Growth Factors	Actual Time			Time In Minutes	
	Start	End	Budgeted Activity	Start	End	Actual Activity	Budget	Actual
1			Leads			Leads		
2			Follow-up			Follow-up		
Total								

Consistency Rate: Total Actual (A)/Budget (B)										
Friday: _____										
	Budgeted Time		Growth Factors	Actual Time				Time In Minutes		
	Start	End	Budgeted Activity	Start	End		Actual Activity	Budget	Actual	
1	10:00am	11:00 am	Leads	10:00am	11:00 am		Leads			
2	11:00am	11:30 am	Follow-up	11:00am	11:20 am		Follow-up			
Total										
Consistency Rate: Total Actual (A)/Budget (B)										

Conversion Rate Scoreboard

Growth Factor	Monday	Tuesday	Wednesday	Thursday	Friday	Week 3
Leads (L)						
Members (M)						
Conversion Rate: M/L						

Quarterly Scoreboard

Pull from week 11 above. The average from Monday to Friday

Growth Factors	W1	W2	W3	W4	W5	W6	W7	W8	W9	W10	W11	W12	W13	Ave/Tot
Consistency %														
Leads														
Members														
Conversion %														

Consistency Rate Scoreboard – Week 12

Monday: _____									
	Budgeted Time		Growth Factors	Actual Time			Time In Minutes		
	Start	End	Budgeted Activity	Start	End	Actual Activity	Budget	Actual	
1			Leads			Leads			
2			Follow-up			Follow-up			
Total									
Consistency Rate: Total Actual (A)/Budget (B)									
Tuesday: _____									
	Budgeted Time		Growth Factors	Actual Time			Time In Minutes		
	Start	End	Budgeted Activity	Start	End	Actual Activity	Budget	Actual	

	Start	End	Budgeted Activity	Start	End	Actual Activity	Budget	Actual
1			Leads			Leads		
2			Follow-up			Follow-up		
Total								
Consistency Rate: Total Actual (A)/Budget (B)								

Wednesday: _____

	Budgeted Time		Growth Factors	Actual Time			Time In Minutes	
	Start	End	Budgeted Activity	Start	End	Actual Activity	Budget	Actual
1			Leads			Leads		
2			Follow-up			Follow-up		
Total								
Consistency Rate: Total Actual (A)/Budget (B)								

Thursday: _____

	Budgeted Time		Growth Factors	Actual Time			Time In Minutes	
	Start	End	Budgeted Activity	Start	End	Actual Activity	Budget	Actual
1			Leads			Leads		
2			Follow-up			Follow-up		
Total								
Consistency Rate: Total Actual (A)/Budget (B)								

Friday: _____

	Budgeted Time		Growth Factors	Actual Time			Time In Minutes	
	Start	End	Budgeted Activity	Start	End	Actual Activity	Budget	Actual
1	10:00am	11:00 am	Leads	10:00am	11:00 am	Leads		
2	11:00am	11:30 am	Follow-up	11:00am	11:20 am	Follow-up		
Total								
Consistency Rate: Total Actual (A)/Budget (B)								

Conversion Rate Scoreboard

Growth Factor	Monday	Tuesday	Wednesday	Thursday	Friday	Week 3
Leads (L)						
Members (M)						
Conversion Rate: M/L						

Quarterly Scoreboard

Pull from week 12 above. The average from Monday to Friday

Growth Factors	W1	W2	W3	W4	W5	W6	W7	W8	W9	W10	W11	W12	W13	Ave/ Tot
Consistency %														
Leads														
Members														
Conversion %														

Consistency Rate Scoreboard – Week 13

Monday: _____

	Budgeted Time		Growth Factors	Actual Time			Time In Minutes	
	Start	End	Budgeted Activity	Start	End	Actual Activity	Budget	Actual
1			Leads			Leads		
2			Follow-up			Follow-up		
Total								

Consistency Rate: Total Actual (A)/Budget (B)

Tuesday: _____

	Budgeted Time		Growth Factors	Actual Time			Time In Minutes	
	Start	End	Budgeted Activity	Start	End	Actual Activity	Budget	Actual
1			Leads			Leads		
2			Follow-up			Follow-up		
Total								

Consistency Rate: Total Actual (A)/Budget (B)

Wednesday: _____

	Budgeted Time		Growth Factors	Actual Time			Time In Minutes	
	Start	End	Budgeted Activity	Start	End	Actual Activity	Budget	Actual
1			Leads			Leads		
2			Follow-up			Follow-up		
Total								

Consistency Rate: Total Actual (A)/Budget (B)

Thursday: _____

	Budgeted Time		Growth Factors	Actual Time			Time In Minutes	
	Start	End	Budgeted Activity	Start	End	Actual Activity	Budget	Actual
1			Leads			Leads		
2			Follow-up			Follow-up		
Total								

Consistency Rate: Total Actual (A)/Budget (B)							
Friday: _____							
	Budgeted Time		Growth Factors	Actual Time			Time In Minutes	
	Start	End	Budgeted Activity	Start	End	Actual Activity	Budget	Actual
1	10:00am	11:00 am	Leads	10:00am	11:00 am	Leads		
2	11:00am	11:30 am	Follow-up	11:00am	11:20 am	Follow-up		
Total								
Consistency Rate: Total Actual (A)/Budget (B)								

Conversion Rate Scoreboard

Growth Factor	Monday	Tuesday	Wednesday	Thursday	Friday	Week 3
Leads (L)						
Members (M)						
Conversion Rate: M/L						

Quarterly Scoreboard

Pull from week 13 above. The average from Monday to Friday

Growth Factors	W1	W2	W3	W4	W5	W6	W7	W8	W9	W10	W11	W12	W13	Ave/Tot
Consistency %														
Leads														
Members														
Conversion %														

Q3 Accountability Scoreboard Templates

Consistency Rate Scoreboard – Week 1

Monday: _____

	Budgeted Time		Growth Factors	Actual Time			Time In Minutes	
	Start	End	Budgeted Activity	Start	End	Actual Activity	Budget	Actual
1			Leads			Leads		
2			Follow-up			Follow-up		
Total								

Consistency Rate: Total Actual (A)/Budget (B)

Tuesday: _____

	Budgeted Time		Growth Factors	Actual Time			Time In Minutes	
	Start	End	Budgeted Activity	Start	End	Actual Activity	Budget	Actual
1			Leads			Leads		
2			Follow-up			Follow-up		
Total								

Consistency Rate: Total Actual (A)/Budget (B)

Wednesday: _____

	Budgeted Time		Growth Factors	Actual Time			Time In Minutes	
	Start	End	Budgeted Activity	Start	End	Actual Activity	Budget	Actual
1			Leads			Leads		
2			Follow-up			Follow-up		
Total								

Consistency Rate: Total Actual (A)/Budget (B)

Thursday: _____

	Budgeted Time		Growth Factors	Actual Time			Time In Minutes	
	Start	End	Budgeted Activity	Start	End	Actual Activity	Budget	Actual
1			Leads			Leads		
2			Follow-up			Follow-up		
Total								

Consistent Profitable Growth Map Workbook

Consistency Rate: Total Actual (A)/Budget (B)							
Friday: _____							
	Budgeted Time		Growth Factors	Actual Time			Time In Minutes	

	Budgeted Time		Growth Factors	Actual Time			Time In Minutes	
	Start	End	Budgeted Activity	Start	End	Actual Activity	Budget	Actual
1	10:00am	11:00 am	Leads	10:00am	11:00 am	Leads		
2	11:00am	11:30 am	Follow-up	11:00am	11:20 am	Follow-up		
Total								
Consistency Rate: Total Actual (A)/Budget (B)								

Conversion Rate Scoreboard

Growth Factor	Monday	Tuesday	Wednesday	Thursday	Friday	Week 3
Leads (L)						
Members (M)						
Conversion Rate: M/L						

Quarterly Scoreboard

Pull from week 1 above. The average from Monday to Friday

Growth Factors	W1	W2	W3	W4	W5	W6	W7	W8	W9	W10	W11	W12	W13	Ave/Tot
Consistency %														
Leads														
Members														
Conversion %														

Consistency Rate Scoreboard – Week 2

Monday: _____							
	Budgeted Time		Growth Factors	Actual Time			Time In Minutes	

	Budgeted Time		Growth Factors	Actual Time			Time In Minutes	
	Start	End	Budgeted Activity	Start	End	Actual Activity	Budget	Actual
1			Leads			Leads		
2			Follow-up			Follow-up		
Total								
Consistency Rate: Total Actual (A)/Budget (B)								

96

Tuesday: _____

	Budgeted Time		Growth Factors	Actual Time			Time In Minutes	
	Start	End	Budgeted Activity	Start	End	Actual Activity	Budget	Actual
1			Leads			Leads		
2			Follow-up			Follow-up		
Total								
Consistency Rate: Total Actual (A)/Budget (B)								

Wednesday: _____

	Budgeted Time		Growth Factors	Actual Time			Time In Minutes	
	Start	End	Budgeted Activity	Start	End	Actual Activity	Budget	Actual
1			Leads			Leads		
2			Follow-up			Follow-up		
Total								
Consistency Rate: Total Actual (A)/Budget (B)								

Thursday: _____

	Budgeted Time		Growth Factors	Actual Time			Time In Minutes	
	Start	End	Budgeted Activity	Start	End	Actual Activity	Budget	Actual
1			Leads			Leads		
2			Follow-up			Follow-up		
Total								
Consistency Rate: Total Actual (A)/Budget (B)								

Friday: _____

	Budgeted Time		Growth Factors	Actual Time			Time In Minutes	
	Start	End	Budgeted Activity	Start	End	Actual Activity	Budget	Actual
1	10:00am	11:00 am	Leads	10:00am	11:00 am	Leads		
2	11:00am	11:30 am	Follow-up	11:00am	11:20 am	Follow-up		
Total								
Consistency Rate: Total Actual (A)/Budget (B)								

Conversion Rate Scoreboard

Growth Factor	Monday	Tuesday	Wednesday	Thursday	Friday	Week 3
Leads (L)						
Members (M)						
Conversion Rate: M/L						

Quarterly Scoreboard

Pull from week 2 above. The average from Monday to Friday

Growth Factors	W1	W2	W3	W4	W5	W6	W7	W8	W9	W10	W11	W12	W13	Ave/Tot
Consistency %														
Leads														
Members														
Conversion %														

Consistency Rate Scoreboard – Week 3

Monday: _____

	Budgeted Time		Growth Factors	Actual Time			Time In Minutes	
	Start	End	Budgeted Activity	Start	End	Actual Activity	Budget	Actual
1			Leads			Leads		
2			Follow-up			Follow-up		
Total								

Consistency Rate: Total Actual (A)/Budget (B)

Tuesday: _____

	Budgeted Time		Growth Factors	Actual Time			Time In Minutes	
	Start	End	Budgeted Activity	Start	End	Actual Activity	Budget	Actual
1			Leads			Leads		
2			Follow-up			Follow-up		
Total								

Consistency Rate: Total Actual (A)/Budget (B)

Wednesday: _____

	Budgeted Time		Growth Factors	Actual Time			Time In Minutes	
	Start	End	Budgeted Activity	Start	End	Actual Activity	Budget	Actual
1			Leads			Leads		
2			Follow-up			Follow-up		
Total								

Consistency Rate: Total Actual (A)/Budget (B)

Thursday: _____

	Budgeted Time		Growth Factors	Actual Time			Time In Minutes	
	Start	End	Budgeted Activity	Start	End	Actual Activity	Budget	Actual
1			Leads			Leads		
2			Follow-up			Follow-up		
Total								

Consistency Rate: Total Actual (A)/Budget (B)								

Friday: _____

	Budgeted Time		Growth Factors	Actual Time			Time In Minutes	
	Start	End	Budgeted Activity	Start	End	Actual Activity	Budget	Actual
1	10:00am	11:00 am	Leads	10:00am	11:00 am	Leads		
2	11:00am	11:30 am	Follow-up	11:00am	11:20 am	Follow-up		
Total								
Consistency Rate: Total Actual (A)/Budget (B)								

Conversion Rate Scoreboard

Growth Factor	Monday	Tuesday	Wednesday	Thursday	Friday	Week 3
Leads (L)						
Members (M)						
Conversion Rate: M/L						

Quarterly Scoreboard

Pull from week 3 above. The average from Monday to Friday

Growth Factors	W1	W2	W3	W4	W5	W6	W7	W8	W9	W10	W11	W12	W13	Ave/Tot
Consistency %														
Leads														
Members														
Conversion %														

Consistency Rate Scoreboard – Week 4

Monday: _____

	Budgeted Time		Growth Factors	Actual Time			Time In Minutes	
	Start	End	Budgeted Activity	Start	End	Actual Activity	Budget	Actual
1			Leads			Leads		
2			Follow-up			Follow-up		
Total								
Consistency Rate: Total Actual (A)/Budget (B)								

Tuesday: _____

	Budgeted Time		Growth Factors	Actual Time			Time In Minutes	
	Start	End	Budgeted Activity	Start	End	Actual Activity	Budget	Actual

	Budgeted Time		Growth Factors	Actual Time			Time In Minutes	
1			Leads			Leads		
2			Follow-up			Follow-up		
Total								
Consistency Rate: Total Actual (A)/Budget (B)								

Wednesday: _____

	Budgeted Time		Growth Factors	Actual Time			Time In Minutes	
	Start	End	Budgeted Activity	Start	End	Actual Activity	Budget	Actual
1			Leads			Leads		
2			Follow-up			Follow-up		
Total								
Consistency Rate: Total Actual (A)/Budget (B)								

Thursday: _____

	Budgeted Time		Growth Factors	Actual Time			Time In Minutes	
	Start	End	Budgeted Activity	Start	End	Actual Activity	Budget	Actual
1			Leads			Leads		
2			Follow-up			Follow-up		
Total								
Consistency Rate: Total Actual (A)/Budget (B)								

Friday: _____

	Budgeted Time		Growth Factors	Actual Time			Time In Minutes	
	Start	End	Budgeted Activity	Start	End	Actual Activity	Budget	Actual
1	10:00am	11:00 am	Leads	10:00am	11:00 am	Leads		
2	11:00am	11:30 am	Follow-up	11:00am	11:20 am	Follow-up		
Total								
Consistency Rate: Total Actual (A)/Budget (B)								

Conversion Rate Scoreboard

Growth Factor	Monday	Tuesday	Wednesday	Thursday	Friday	Week 3
Leads (L)						
Members (M)						
Conversion Rate: M/L						

Quarterly Scoreboard

Pull from week 4 above. The average from Monday to Friday

Growth Factors	W1	W2	W3	W4	W5	W6	W7	W8	W9	W10	W11	W12	W13	Ave/ Tot
Consistency %														
Leads														
Members														
Conversion %														

Consistency Rate Scoreboard – Week 5

Monday: _____

	Budgeted Time		Growth Factors	Actual Time				Time In Minutes	
	Start	End	Budgeted Activity	Start	End	Actual Activity		Budget	Actual
1			Leads			Leads			
2			Follow-up			Follow-up			
Total									

Consistency Rate: Total Actual (A)/Budget (B)

Tuesday: _____

	Budgeted Time		Growth Factors	Actual Time				Time In Minutes	
	Start	End	Budgeted Activity	Start	End	Actual Activity		Budget	Actual
1			Leads			Leads			
2			Follow-up			Follow-up			
Total									

Consistency Rate: Total Actual (A)/Budget (B)

Wednesday: _____

	Budgeted Time		Growth Factors	Actual Time				Time In Minutes	
	Start	End	Budgeted Activity	Start	End	Actual Activity		Budget	Actual
1			Leads			Leads			
2			Follow-up			Follow-up			
Total									

Consistency Rate: Total Actual (A)/Budget (B)

Thursday: _____

	Budgeted Time		Growth Factors	Actual Time				Time In Minutes	
	Start	End	Budgeted Activity	Start	End	Actual Activity		Budget	Actual
1			Leads			Leads			
2			Follow-up			Follow-up			
Total									

Consistency Rate: Total Actual (A)/Budget (B)							
Friday: _____							
	Budgeted Time		Growth Factors	Actual Time			Time In Minutes	
	Start	End	Budgeted Activity	Start	End	Actual Activity	Budget	Actual
1	10:00am	11:00 am	Leads	10:00am	11:00 am	Leads		
2	11:00am	11:30 am	Follow-up	11:00am	11:20 am	Follow-up		
Total								
Consistency Rate: Total Actual (A)/Budget (B)								

Conversion Rate Scoreboard

Growth Factor	Monday	Tuesday	Wednesday	Thursday	Friday	Week 3
Leads (L)						
Members (M)						
Conversion Rate: M/L						

Quarterly Scoreboard

Pull from week 5 above. The average from Monday to Friday

Growth Factors	W1	W2	W3	W4	W5	W6	W7	W8	W9	W10	W11	W12	W13	Ave/Tot
Consistency %														
Leads														
Members														
Conversion %														

Consistency Rate Scoreboard – Week 6

Monday: _____							
	Budgeted Time		Growth Factors	Actual Time			Time In Minutes	
	Start	End	Budgeted Activity	Start	End	Actual Activity	Budget	Actual
1			Leads			Leads		
2			Follow-up			Follow-up		
Total								

Consistency Rate: Total Actual (A)/Budget (B)							

Tuesday: _____

	Budgeted Time		Growth Factors	Actual Time			Time In Minutes	
	Start	End	Budgeted Activity	Start	End	Actual Activity	Budget	Actual
1			Leads			Leads		
2			Follow-up			Follow-up		
Total								

Consistency Rate: Total Actual (A)/Budget (B)							

Wednesday: _____

	Budgeted Time		Growth Factors	Actual Time			Time In Minutes	
	Start	End	Budgeted Activity	Start	End	Actual Activity	Budget	Actual
1			Leads			Leads		
2			Follow-up			Follow-up		
Total								

Consistency Rate: Total Actual (A)/Budget (B)							

Thursday: _____

	Budgeted Time		Growth Factors	Actual Time			Time In Minutes	
	Start	End	Budgeted Activity	Start	End	Actual Activity	Budget	Actual
1			Leads			Leads		
2			Follow-up			Follow-up		
Total								

Consistency Rate: Total Actual (A)/Budget (B)							

Friday: _____

	Budgeted Time		Growth Factors	Actual Time			Time In Minutes	
	Start	End	Budgeted Activity	Start	End	Actual Activity	Budget	Actual
1	10:00am	11:00 am	Leads	10:00am	11:00 am	Leads		
2	11:00am	11:30 am	Follow-up	11:00am	11:20 am	Follow-up		
Total								

Consistency Rate: Total Actual (A)/Budget (B)							

Conversion Rate Scoreboard

Growth Factor	Monday	Tuesday	Wednesday	Thursday	Friday	Week 3
Leads (L)						
Members (M)						
Conversion Rate: M/L						

Quarterly Scoreboard

Pull from week 6 above. The average from Monday to Friday

Growth Factors	W1	W2	W3	W4	W5	W6	W7	W8	W9	W10	W11	W12	W13	Ave/ Tot
Consistency %														
Leads														
Members														
Conversion %														

Consistency Rate Scoreboard – Week 7

Monday: _____

	Budgeted Time		Growth Factors	Actual Time			Time In Minutes	
	Start	End	Budgeted Activity	Start	End	Actual Activity	Budget	Actual
1			Leads			Leads		
2			Follow-up			Follow-up		
Total								

Consistency Rate: Total Actual (A)/Budget (B)	

Tuesday: _____

	Budgeted Time		Growth Factors	Actual Time			Time In Minutes	
	Start	End	Budgeted Activity	Start	End	Actual Activity	Budget	Actual
1			Leads			Leads		
2			Follow-up			Follow-up		
Total								

Consistency Rate: Total Actual (A)/Budget (B)	

Wednesday: _____

	Budgeted Time		Growth Factors	Actual Time			Time In Minutes	
	Start	End	Budgeted Activity	Start	End	Actual Activity	Budget	Actual
1			Leads			Leads		
2			Follow-up			Follow-up		
Total								

Consistency Rate: Total Actual (A)/Budget (B)	

Thursday: _____

	Budgeted Time		Growth Factors	Actual Time			Time In Minutes	
	Start	End	Budgeted Activity	Start	End	Actual Activity	Budget	Actual
1			Leads			Leads		
2			Follow-up			Follow-up		
Total								

Consistency Rate: Total Actual (A)/Budget (B)							

Friday: _____

	Budgeted Time		Growth Factors	Actual Time			Time In Minutes	
	Start	End	Budgeted Activity	Start	End	Actual Activity	Budget	Actual
1	10:00am	11:00 am	Leads	10:00am	11:00 am	Leads		
2	11:00am	11:30 am	Follow-up	11:00am	11:20 am	Follow-up		
Total								
Consistency Rate: Total Actual (A)/Budget (B)								

Conversion Rate Scoreboard

Growth Factor	Monday	Tuesday	Wednesday	Thursday	Friday	Week 3
Leads (L)						
Members (M)						
Conversion Rate: M/L						

Quarterly Scoreboard

Pull from week 7 above. The average from Monday to Friday

Growth Factors	W1	W2	W3	W4	W5	W6	W7	W8	W9	W10	W11	W12	W13	Ave/Tot
Consistency %														
Leads														
Members														
Conversion %														

Consistency Rate Scoreboard – Week 8

Monday: _____

	Budgeted Time		Growth Factors	Actual Time			Time In Minutes	
	Start	End	Budgeted Activity	Start	End	Actual Activity	Budget	Actual
1			Leads			Leads		
2			Follow-up			Follow-up		
Total								
Consistency Rate: Total Actual (A)/Budget (B)								

Tuesday: _____

	Budgeted Time	Growth Factors	Actual Time		Time In Minutes

	Start	End	Budgeted Activity	Start	End	Actual Activity	Budget	Actual
1			Leads			Leads		
2			Follow-up			Follow-up		
Total								

Consistency Rate: Total Actual (A)/Budget (B)

Wednesday: _____

	Budgeted Time		Growth Factors	Actual Time			Time In Minutes	
	Start	End	Budgeted Activity	Start	End	Actual Activity	Budget	Actual
1			Leads			Leads		
2			Follow-up			Follow-up		
Total								

Consistency Rate: Total Actual (A)/Budget (B)

Thursday: _____

	Budgeted Time		Growth Factors	Actual Time			Time In Minutes	
	Start	End	Budgeted Activity	Start	End	Actual Activity	Budget	Actual
1			Leads			Leads		
2			Follow-up			Follow-up		
Total								

Consistency Rate: Total Actual (A)/Budget (B)

Friday: _____

	Budgeted Time		Growth Factors	Actual Time			Time In Minutes	
	Start	End	Budgeted Activity	Start	End	Actual Activity	Budget	Actual
1	10:00am	11:00 am	Leads	10:00am	11:00 am	Leads		
2	11:00am	11:30 am	Follow-up	11:00am	11:20 am	Follow-up		
Total								

Consistency Rate: Total Actual (A)/Budget (B)

Conversion Rate Scoreboard

Growth Factor	Monday	Tuesday	Wednesday	Thursday	Friday	Week 3
Leads (L)						
Members (M)						
Conversion Rate: M/L						

Quarterly Scoreboard

Pull from week 8 above. The average from Monday to Friday

Growth Factors	W1	W2	W3	W4	W5	W6	W7	W8	W9	W10	W11	W12	W13	Ave/Tot
Consistency %														
Leads														
Members														
Conversion %														

Consistency Rate Scoreboard – Week 9

Monday: _____

	Budgeted Time		Growth Factors	Actual Time			Time In Minutes	
	Start	End	Budgeted Activity	Start	End	Actual Activity	Budget	Actual
1			Leads			Leads		
2			Follow-up			Follow-up		
Total								

Consistency Rate: Total Actual (A)/Budget (B)

Tuesday: _____

	Budgeted Time		Growth Factors	Actual Time			Time In Minutes	
	Start	End	Budgeted Activity	Start	End	Actual Activity	Budget	Actual
1			Leads			Leads		
2			Follow-up			Follow-up		
Total								

Consistency Rate: Total Actual (A)/Budget (B)

Wednesday: _____

	Budgeted Time		Growth Factors	Actual Time			Time In Minutes	
	Start	End	Budgeted Activity	Start	End	Actual Activity	Budget	Actual
1			Leads			Leads		
2			Follow-up			Follow-up		
Total								

Consistency Rate: Total Actual (A)/Budget (B)

Thursday: _____

	Budgeted Time		Growth Factors	Actual Time			Time In Minutes	
	Start	End	Budgeted Activity	Start	End	Actual Activity	Budget	Actual
1			Leads			Leads		
2			Follow-up			Follow-up		
Total								

Consistency Rate: Total Actual (A)/Budget (B)							
Friday: _____							
	Budgeted Time		Growth Factors	Actual Time			Time In Minutes	
	Start	End	Budgeted Activity	Start	End	Actual Activity	Budget	Actual
1	10:00am	11:00 am	Leads	10:00am	11:00 am	Leads		
2	11:00am	11:30 am	Follow-up	11:00am	11:20 am	Follow-up		
Total								
Consistency Rate: Total Actual (A)/Budget (B)								

Conversion Rate Scoreboard

Growth Factor	Monday	Tuesday	Wednesday	Thursday	Friday	Week 3
Leads (L)						
Members (M)						
Conversion Rate: M/L						

Quarterly Scoreboard

Pull from week 9 above. The average from Monday to Friday

Growth Factors	W1	W2	W3	W4	W5	W6	W7	W8	W9	W10	W11	W12	W13	Ave/Tot
Consistency %														
Leads														
Members														
Conversion %														

Consistency Rate Scoreboard – Week 10

Monday: _____							
	Budgeted Time		Growth Factors	Actual Time			Time In Minutes	
	Start	End	Budgeted Activity	Start	End	Actual Activity	Budget	Actual
1			Leads			Leads		
2			Follow-up			Follow-up		
Total								
Consistency Rate: Total Actual (A)/Budget (B)								

Tuesday: _____

	Budgeted Time		Growth Factors	Actual Time			Time In Minutes	
	Start	End	Budgeted Activity	Start	End	Actual Activity	Budget	Actual
1			Leads			Leads		
2			Follow-up			Follow-up		
Total								
Consistency Rate: Total Actual (A)/Budget (B)								

Wednesday: _____

	Budgeted Time		Growth Factors	Actual Time			Time In Minutes	
	Start	End	Budgeted Activity	Start	End	Actual Activity	Budget	Actual
1			Leads			Leads		
2			Follow-up			Follow-up		
Total								
Consistency Rate: Total Actual (A)/Budget (B)								

Thursday: _____

	Budgeted Time		Growth Factors	Actual Time			Time In Minutes	
	Start	End	Budgeted Activity	Start	End	Actual Activity	Budget	Actual
1			Leads			Leads		
2			Follow-up			Follow-up		
Total								
Consistency Rate: Total Actual (A)/Budget (B)								

Friday: _____

	Budgeted Time		Growth Factors	Actual Time			Time In Minutes	
	Start	End	Budgeted Activity	Start	End	Actual Activity	Budget	Actual
1	10:00am	11:00 am	Leads	10:00am	11:00 am	Leads		
2	11:00am	11:30 am	Follow-up	11:00am	11:20 am	Follow-up		
Total								
Consistency Rate: Total Actual (A)/Budget (B)								

Conversion Rate Scoreboard

Growth Factor	Monday	Tuesday	Wednesday	Thursday	Friday	Week 3
Leads (L)						
Members (M)						
Conversion Rate: M/L						

Quarterly Scoreboard

Pull from week 10 above. The average from Monday to Friday

Growth Factors	W1	W2	W3	W4	W5	W6	W7	W8	W9	W10	W11	W12	W13	Ave/Tot
Consistency %														
Leads														
Members														
Conversion %														

Consistency Rate Scoreboard – Week 11

Monday: _____

	Budgeted Time		Growth Factors	Actual Time			Time In Minutes	
	Start	End	Budgeted Activity	Start	End	Actual Activity	Budget	Actual
1			Leads			Leads		
2			Follow-up			Follow-up		
Total								

Consistency Rate: Total Actual (A)/Budget (B)

Tuesday: _____

	Budgeted Time		Growth Factors	Actual Time			Time In Minutes	
	Start	End	Budgeted Activity	Start	End	Actual Activity	Budget	Actual
1			Leads			Leads		
2			Follow-up			Follow-up		
Total								

Consistency Rate: Total Actual (A)/Budget (B)

Wednesday: _____

	Budgeted Time		Growth Factors	Actual Time			Time In Minutes	
	Start	End	Budgeted Activity	Start	End	Actual Activity	Budget	Actual
1			Leads			Leads		
2			Follow-up			Follow-up		
Total								

Consistency Rate: Total Actual (A)/Budget (B)

Thursday: _____

	Budgeted Time		Growth Factors	Actual Time			Time In Minutes	
	Start	End	Budgeted Activity	Start	End	Actual Activity	Budget	Actual
1			Leads			Leads		
2			Follow-up			Follow-up		
Total								

Consistency Rate: Total Actual (A)/Budget (B)								

Friday: _____

	Budgeted Time		Growth Factors	Actual Time			Time In Minutes	
	Start	End	Budgeted Activity	Start	End	Actual Activity	Budget	Actual
1	10:00am	11:00 am	Leads	10:00am	11:00 am	Leads		
2	11:00am	11:30 am	Follow-up	11:00am	11:20 am	Follow-up		
Total								
Consistency Rate: Total Actual (A)/Budget (B)								

Conversion Rate Scoreboard

Growth Factor	Monday	Tuesday	Wednesday	Thursday	Friday	Week 3
Leads (L)						
Members (M)						
Conversion Rate: M/L						

Quarterly Scoreboard

Pull from week 11 above. The average from Monday to Friday

Growth Factors	W1	W2	W3	W4	W5	W6	W7	W8	W9	W10	W11	W12	W13	Ave/ Tot
Consistency %														
Leads														
Members														
Conversion %														

Consistency Rate Scoreboard – Week 12

Monday: _____

	Budgeted Time		Growth Factors	Actual Time			Time In Minutes	
	Start	End	Budgeted Activity	Start	End	Actual Activity	Budget	Actual
1			Leads			Leads		
2			Follow-up			Follow-up		
Total								
Consistency Rate: Total Actual (A)/Budget (B)								

Tuesday: _____

	Budgeted Time	Growth Factors	Actual Time		Time In Minutes

	Start	End	Budgeted Activity	Start	End	Actual Activity	Budget	Actual
1			Leads			Leads		
2			Follow-up			Follow-up		
Total								
Consistency Rate: Total Actual (A)/Budget (B)								

Wednesday: _____

	Budgeted Time		Growth Factors	Actual Time			Time In Minutes	
	Start	End	Budgeted Activity	Start	End	Actual Activity	Budget	Actual
1			Leads			Leads		
2			Follow-up			Follow-up		
Total								
Consistency Rate: Total Actual (A)/Budget (B)								

Thursday: _____

	Budgeted Time		Growth Factors	Actual Time			Time In Minutes	
	Start	End	Budgeted Activity	Start	End	Actual Activity	Budget	Actual
1			Leads			Leads		
2			Follow-up			Follow-up		
Total								
Consistency Rate: Total Actual (A)/Budget (B)								

Friday: _____

	Budgeted Time		Growth Factors	Actual Time			Time In Minutes	
	Start	End	Budgeted Activity	Start	End	Actual Activity	Budget	Actual
1	10:00am	11:00 am	Leads	10:00am	11:00 am	Leads		
2	11:00am	11:30 am	Follow-up	11:00am	11:20 am	Follow-up		
Total								
Consistency Rate: Total Actual (A)/Budget (B)								

Conversion Rate Scoreboard

Growth Factor	Monday	Tuesday	Wednesday	Thursday	Friday	Week 3
Leads (L)						
Members (M)						
Conversion Rate: M/L						

Quarterly Scoreboard

Pull from week 12 above. The average from Monday to Friday

Growth Factors	W1	W2	W3	W4	W5	W6	W7	W8	W9	W10	W11	W12	W13	Ave/Tot
Consistency %														
Leads														
Members														
Conversion %														

Consistency Rate Scoreboard – Week 13

Monday: _____

	Budgeted Time		Growth Factors	Actual Time				Time In Minutes	
	Start	End	Budgeted Activity	Start	End		Actual Activity	Budget	Actual
1			Leads				Leads		
2			Follow-up				Follow-up		
Total									

Consistency Rate: Total Actual (A)/Budget (B)

Tuesday: _____

	Budgeted Time		Growth Factors	Actual Time				Time In Minutes	
	Start	End	Budgeted Activity	Start	End		Actual Activity	Budget	Actual
1			Leads				Leads		
2			Follow-up				Follow-up		
Total									

Consistency Rate: Total Actual (A)/Budget (B)

Wednesday: _____

	Budgeted Time		Growth Factors	Actual Time				Time In Minutes	
	Start	End	Budgeted Activity	Start	End		Actual Activity	Budget	Actual
1			Leads				Leads		
2			Follow-up				Follow-up		
Total									

Consistency Rate: Total Actual (A)/Budget (B)

Thursday: _____

	Budgeted Time		Growth Factors	Actual Time				Time In Minutes	
	Start	End	Budgeted Activity	Start	End		Actual Activity	Budget	Actual
1			Leads				Leads		
2			Follow-up				Follow-up		
Total									

	Consistency Rate: Total Actual (A)/Budget (B)							

Friday: _____

	Budgeted Time		Growth Factors	Actual Time			Time In Minutes	
	Start	End	Budgeted Activity	Start	End	Actual Activity	Budget	Actual
1	10:00am	11:00 am	Leads	10:00am	11:00 am	Leads		
2	11:00am	11:30 am	Follow-up	11:00am	11:20 am	Follow-up		
Total								
Consistency Rate: Total Actual (A)/Budget (B)								

Conversion Rate Scoreboard

Growth Factor	Monday	Tuesday	Wednesday	Thursday	Friday	Week 3
Leads (L)						
Members (M)						
Conversion Rate: M/L						

Quarterly Scoreboard

Pull from week 13 above. The average from Monday to Friday

Growth Factors	W1	W2	W3	W4	W5	W6	W7	W8	W9	W10	W11	W12	W13	Ave/Tot
Consistency %														
Leads														
Members														
Conversion %														

Q4 Accountability Scoreboard Templates

Consistency Rate Scoreboard – Week 1

Monday: _____

	Budgeted Time		Growth Factors	Actual Time			Time In Minutes	
	Start	End	Budgeted Activity	Start	End	Actual Activity	Budget	Actual
1			Leads			Leads		
2			Follow-up			Follow-up		
Total								

Consistency Rate: Total Actual (A)/Budget (B)

Tuesday: _____

	Budgeted Time		Growth Factors	Actual Time			Time In Minutes	
	Start	End	Budgeted Activity	Start	End	Actual Activity	Budget	Actual
1			Leads			Leads		
2			Follow-up			Follow-up		
Total								

Consistency Rate: Total Actual (A)/Budget (B)

Wednesday: _____

	Budgeted Time		Growth Factors	Actual Time			Time In Minutes	
	Start	End	Budgeted Activity	Start	End	Actual Activity	Budget	Actual
1			Leads			Leads		
2			Follow-up			Follow-up		
Total								

Consistency Rate: Total Actual (A)/Budget (B)

Thursday: _____

	Budgeted Time		Growth Factors	Actual Time			Time In Minutes	
	Start	End	Budgeted Activity	Start	End	Actual Activity	Budget	Actual
1			Leads			Leads		
2			Follow-up			Follow-up		
Total								

Consistency Rate: Total Actual (A)/Budget (B)							
Friday: _____							
	Budgeted Time		Growth Factors	Actual Time			Time In Minutes	
	Start	End	Budgeted Activity	Start	End	Actual Activity	Budget	Actual
1	10:00am	11:00 am	Leads	10:00am	11:00 am	Leads		
2	11:00am	11:30 am	Follow-up	11:00am	11:20 am	Follow-up		
Total								
Consistency Rate: Total Actual (A)/Budget (B)								

Conversion Rate Scoreboard

Growth Factor	Monday	Tuesday	Wednesday	Thursday	Friday	Week 3
Leads (L)						
Members (M)						
Conversion Rate: M/L						

Quarterly Scoreboard

Pull from week 1 above. The average from Monday to Friday

Growth Factors	W1	W2	W3	W4	W5	W6	W7	W8	W9	W10	W11	W12	W13	Ave/Tot
Consistency %														
Leads														
Members														
Conversion %														

Consistency Rate Scoreboard – Week 2

Monday: _____								
	Budgeted Time		Growth Factors	Actual Time			Time In Minutes	
	Start	End	Budgeted Activity	Start	End	Actual Activity	Budget	Actual
1			Leads			Leads		
2			Follow-up			Follow-up		
Total								

Consistency Rate: Total Actual (A)/Budget (B)								
Tuesday: _____								
	Budgeted Time		Growth Factors	Actual Time			Time In Minutes	
	Start	End	Budgeted Activity	Start	End	Actual Activity	Budget	Actual
1			Leads			Leads		
2			Follow-up			Follow-up		
Total								
Consistency Rate: Total Actual (A)/Budget (B)								
Wednesday: _____								
	Budgeted Time		Growth Factors	Actual Time			Time In Minutes	
	Start	End	Budgeted Activity	Start	End	Actual Activity	Budget	Actual
1			Leads			Leads		
2			Follow-up			Follow-up		
Total								
Consistency Rate: Total Actual (A)/Budget (B)								
Thursday: _____								
	Budgeted Time		Growth Factors	Actual Time			Time In Minutes	
	Start	End	Budgeted Activity	Start	End	Actual Activity	Budget	Actual
1			Leads			Leads		
2			Follow-up			Follow-up		
Total								
Consistency Rate: Total Actual (A)/Budget (B)								
Friday: _____								
	Budgeted Time		Growth Factors	Actual Time			Time In Minutes	
	Start	End	Budgeted Activity	Start	End	Actual Activity	Budget	Actual
1	10:00am	11:00 am	Leads	10:00am	11:00 am	Leads		
2	11:00am	11:30 am	Follow-up	11:00am	11:20 am	Follow-up		
Total								
Consistency Rate: Total Actual (A)/Budget (B)								

Conversion Rate Scoreboard

Growth Factor	Monday	Tuesday	Wednesday	Thursday	Friday	Week 3
Leads (L)						
Members (M)						
Conversion Rate: M/L						

Quarterly Scoreboard

Pull from week 2 above. The average from Monday to Friday

Growth Factors	W1	W2	W3	W4	W5	W6	W7	W8	W9	W10	W11	W12	W13	Ave/Tot
Consistency %														
Leads														
Members														
Conversion %														

Consistency Rate Scoreboard – Week 3

Monday: _____

	Budgeted Time		Growth Factors	Actual Time			Time In Minutes	
	Start	End	Budgeted Activity	Start	End	Actual Activity	Budget	Actual
1			Leads			Leads		
2			Follow-up			Follow-up		
Total								

Consistency Rate: Total Actual (A)/Budget (B)

Tuesday: _____

	Budgeted Time		Growth Factors	Actual Time			Time In Minutes	
	Start	End	Budgeted Activity	Start	End	Actual Activity	Budget	Actual
1			Leads			Leads		
2			Follow-up			Follow-up		
Total								

Consistency Rate: Total Actual (A)/Budget (B)

Wednesday: _____

	Budgeted Time		Growth Factors	Actual Time			Time In Minutes	
	Start	End	Budgeted Activity	Start	End	Actual Activity	Budget	Actual
1			Leads			Leads		
2			Follow-up			Follow-up		
Total								

Consistency Rate: Total Actual (A)/Budget (B)

Thursday: _____

	Budgeted Time		Growth Factors	Actual Time			Time In Minutes	
	Start	End	Budgeted Activity	Start	End	Actual Activity	Budget	Actual
1			Leads			Leads		
2			Follow-up			Follow-up		
Total								

	Consistency Rate: Total Actual (A)/Budget (B)							

Friday: _____

	Budgeted Time		Growth Factors	Actual Time			Time In Minutes	
	Start	End	Budgeted Activity	Start	End	Actual Activity	Budget	Actual
1	10:00am	11:00 am	Leads	10:00am	11:00 am	Leads		
2	11:00am	11:30 am	Follow-up	11:00am	11:20 am	Follow-up		
Total								
Consistency Rate: Total Actual (A)/Budget (B)								

Conversion Rate Scoreboard

Growth Factor	Monday	Tuesday	Wednesday	Thursday	Friday	Week 3
Leads (L)						
Members (M)						
Conversion Rate: M/L						

Quarterly Scoreboard

Pull from week 3 above. The average from Monday to Friday

Growth Factors	W1	W2	W3	W4	W5	W6	W7	W8	W9	W10	W11	W12	W13	Ave/Tot
Consistency %														
Leads														
Members														
Conversion %														

Consistency Rate Scoreboard – Week 4

Monday: _____

	Budgeted Time		Growth Factors	Actual Time			Time In Minutes	
	Start	End	Budgeted Activity	Start	End	Actual Activity	Budget	Actual
1			Leads			Leads		
2			Follow-up			Follow-up		
Total								
Consistency Rate: Total Actual (A)/Budget (B)								

Tuesday: _____

	Budgeted Time		Growth Factors	Actual Time			Time In Minutes	
	Start	End	Budgeted Activity	Start	End	Actual Activity	Budget	Actual

	Budgeted Time		Growth Factors	Actual Time			Time In Minutes	
1			Leads			Leads		
2			Follow-up			Follow-up		
Total								
Consistency Rate: Total Actual (A)/Budget (B)								

Wednesday: _____

	Budgeted Time		Growth Factors	Actual Time			Time In Minutes	
	Start	End	Budgeted Activity	Start	End	Actual Activity	Budget	Actual
1			Leads			Leads		
2			Follow-up			Follow-up		
Total								
Consistency Rate: Total Actual (A)/Budget (B)								

Thursday: _____

	Budgeted Time		Growth Factors	Actual Time			Time In Minutes	
	Start	End	Budgeted Activity	Start	End	Actual Activity	Budget	Actual
1			Leads			Leads		
2			Follow-up			Follow-up		
Total								
Consistency Rate: Total Actual (A)/Budget (B)								

Friday: _____

	Budgeted Time		Growth Factors	Actual Time			Time In Minutes	
	Start	End	Budgeted Activity	Start	End	Actual Activity	Budget	Actual
1	10:00am	11:00 am	Leads	10:00am	11:00 am	Leads		
2	11:00am	11:30 am	Follow-up	11:00am	11:20 am	Follow-up		
Total								
Consistency Rate: Total Actual (A)/Budget (B)								

Conversion Rate Scoreboard

Growth Factor	Monday	Tuesday	Wednesday	Thursday	Friday	Week 3
Leads (L)						
Members (M)						
Conversion Rate: M/L						

Quarterly Scoreboard

Pull from week 4 above. The average from Monday to Friday

Growth Factors	W1	W2	W3	W4	W5	W6	W7	W8	W9	W10	W11	W12	W13	Ave/Tot
Consistency %														
Leads														
Members														
Conversion %														

Consistency Rate Scoreboard – Week 5

Monday: _____

	Budgeted Time		Growth Factors	Actual Time			Time In Minutes	
	Start	End	Budgeted Activity	Start	End	Actual Activity	Budget	Actual
1			Leads			Leads		
2			Follow-up			Follow-up		
Total								

Consistency Rate: Total Actual (A)/Budget (B)

Tuesday: _____

	Budgeted Time		Growth Factors	Actual Time			Time In Minutes	
	Start	End	Budgeted Activity	Start	End	Actual Activity	Budget	Actual
1			Leads			Leads		
2			Follow-up			Follow-up		
Total								

Consistency Rate: Total Actual (A)/Budget (B)

Wednesday: _____

	Budgeted Time		Growth Factors	Actual Time			Time In Minutes	
	Start	End	Budgeted Activity	Start	End	Actual Activity	Budget	Actual
1			Leads			Leads		
2			Follow-up			Follow-up		
Total								

Consistency Rate: Total Actual (A)/Budget (B)

Thursday: _____

	Budgeted Time		Growth Factors	Actual Time			Time In Minutes	
	Start	End	Budgeted Activity	Start	End	Actual Activity	Budget	Actual
1			Leads			Leads		
2			Follow-up			Follow-up		
Total								

Consistency Rate: Total Actual (A)/Budget (B)							
Friday: _____							
	Budgeted Time		Growth Factors	Actual Time			Time In Minutes	

	Start	End	Budgeted Activity	Start	End	Actual Activity	Budget	Actual
1	10:00am	11:00 am	Leads	10:00am	11:00 am	Leads		
2	11:00am	11:30 am	Follow-up	11:00am	11:20 am	Follow-up		
Total								
Consistency Rate: Total Actual (A)/Budget (B)								

Conversion Rate Scoreboard

Growth Factor	Monday	Tuesday	Wednesday	Thursday	Friday	Week 3
Leads (L)						
Members (M)						
Conversion Rate: M/L						

Quarterly Scoreboard

Pull from week 5 above. The average from Monday to Friday

Growth Factors	W1	W2	W3	W4	W5	W6	W7	W8	W9	W10	W11	W12	W13	Ave/Tot
Consistency %														
Leads														
Members														
Conversion %														

Consistency Rate Scoreboard – Week 6

Monday: _____							
	Budgeted Time		Growth Factors	Actual Time			Time In Minutes	

	Start	End	Budgeted Activity	Start	End	Actual Activity	Budget	Actual
1			Leads			Leads		
2			Follow-up			Follow-up		
Total								

Consistency Rate: Total Actual (A)/Budget (B)								

Tuesday: _____

	Budgeted Time		Growth Factors	Actual Time			Time In Minutes	
	Start	End	Budgeted Activity	Start	End	Actual Activity	Budget	Actual
1			Leads			Leads		
2			Follow-up			Follow-up		
Total								

Consistency Rate: Total Actual (A)/Budget (B)								

Wednesday: _____

	Budgeted Time		Growth Factors	Actual Time			Time In Minutes	
	Start	End	Budgeted Activity	Start	End	Actual Activity	Budget	Actual
1			Leads			Leads		
2			Follow-up			Follow-up		
Total								

Consistency Rate: Total Actual (A)/Budget (B)								

Thursday: _____

	Budgeted Time		Growth Factors	Actual Time			Time In Minutes	
	Start	End	Budgeted Activity	Start	End	Actual Activity	Budget	Actual
1			Leads			Leads		
2			Follow-up			Follow-up		
Total								

Consistency Rate: Total Actual (A)/Budget (B)								

Friday: _____

	Budgeted Time		Growth Factors	Actual Time			Time In Minutes	
	Start	End	Budgeted Activity	Start	End	Actual Activity	Budget	Actual
1	10:00am	11:00 am	Leads	10:00am	11:00 am	Leads		
2	11:00am	11:30 am	Follow-up	11:00am	11:20 am	Follow-up		
Total								

Consistency Rate: Total Actual (A)/Budget (B)								

Conversion Rate Scoreboard

Growth Factor	Monday	Tuesday	Wednesday	Thursday	Friday	Week 3
Leads (L)						
Members (M)						
Conversion Rate: M/L						

Quarterly Scoreboard

Pull from week 6 above. The average from Monday to Friday

Growth Factors	W1	W2	W3	W4	W5	W6	W7	W8	W9	W10	W11	W12	W13	Ave/Tot
Consistency %														
Leads														
Members														
Conversion %														

Consistency Rate Scoreboard – Week 7

Monday: _____

	Budgeted Time		Growth Factors	Actual Time			Time In Minutes	
	Start	End	Budgeted Activity	Start	End	Actual Activity	Budget	Actual
1			Leads			Leads		
2			Follow-up			Follow-up		
Total								

Consistency Rate: Total Actual (A)/Budget (B)

Tuesday: _____

	Budgeted Time		Growth Factors	Actual Time			Time In Minutes	
	Start	End	Budgeted Activity	Start	End	Actual Activity	Budget	Actual
1			Leads			Leads		
2			Follow-up			Follow-up		
Total								

Consistency Rate: Total Actual (A)/Budget (B)

Wednesday: _____

	Budgeted Time		Growth Factors	Actual Time			Time In Minutes	
	Start	End	Budgeted Activity	Start	End	Actual Activity	Budget	Actual
1			Leads			Leads		
2			Follow-up			Follow-up		
Total								

Consistency Rate: Total Actual (A)/Budget (B)

Thursday: _____

	Budgeted Time		Growth Factors	Actual Time			Time In Minutes	
	Start	End	Budgeted Activity	Start	End	Actual Activity	Budget	Actual
1			Leads			Leads		
2			Follow-up			Follow-up		
Total								

Consistency Rate: Total Actual (A)/Budget (B)								
Friday: _____								
	Budgeted Time		Growth Factors	Actual Time			Time In Minutes	
	Start	End	Budgeted Activity	Start	End	Actual Activity	Budget	Actual
1	10:00am	11:00 am	Leads	10:00am	11:00 am	Leads		
2	11:00am	11:30 am	Follow-up	11:00am	11:20 am	Follow-up		
Total								
Consistency Rate: Total Actual (A)/Budget (B)								

Conversion Rate Scoreboard

Growth Factor	Monday	Tuesday	Wednesday	Thursday	Friday	Week 3
Leads (L)						
Members (M)						
Conversion Rate: M/L						

Quarterly Scoreboard

Pull from week 7 above. The average from Monday to Friday

Growth Factors	W1	W2	W3	W4	W5	W6	W7	W8	W9	W10	W11	W12	W13	Ave/Tot
Consistency %														
Leads														
Members														
Conversion %														

Consistency Rate Scoreboard – Week 8

Monday: _____								
	Budgeted Time		Growth Factors	Actual Time			Time In Minutes	
	Start	End	Budgeted Activity	Start	End	Actual Activity	Budget	Actual
1			Leads			Leads		
2			Follow-up			Follow-up		
Total								
Consistency Rate: Total Actual (A)/Budget (B)								
Tuesday: _____								
	Budgeted Time		Growth Factors	Actual Time			Time In Minutes	
	Start	End	Budgeted Activity	Start	End	Actual Activity	Budget	Actual

1			Leads			Leads		
2			Follow-up			Follow-up		
Total								
Consistency Rate: Total Actual (A)/Budget (B)								

Wednesday: _____

	Budgeted Time		Growth Factors	Actual Time			Time In Minutes	
	Start	End	Budgeted Activity	Start	End	Actual Activity	Budget	Actual
1			Leads			Leads		
2			Follow-up			Follow-up		
Total								
Consistency Rate: Total Actual (A)/Budget (B)								

Thursday: _____

	Budgeted Time		Growth Factors	Actual Time			Time In Minutes	
	Start	End	Budgeted Activity	Start	End	Actual Activity	Budget	Actual
1			Leads			Leads		
2			Follow-up			Follow-up		
Total								
Consistency Rate: Total Actual (A)/Budget (B)								

Friday: _____

	Budgeted Time		Growth Factors	Actual Time			Time In Minutes	
	Start	End	Budgeted Activity	Start	End	Actual Activity	Budget	Actual
1	10:00am	11:00 am	Leads	10:00am	11:00 am	Leads		
2	11:00am	11:30 am	Follow-up	11:00am	11:20 am	Follow-up		
Total								
Consistency Rate: Total Actual (A)/Budget (B)								

Conversion Rate Scoreboard

Growth Factor	Monday	Tuesday	Wednesday	Thursday	Friday	Week 3
Leads (L)						
Members (M)						
Conversion Rate: M/L						

Quarterly Scoreboard

Pull from week 8 above. The average from Monday to Friday

Growth Factors	W1	W2	W3	W4	W5	W6	W7	W8	W9	W10	W11	W12	W13	Ave/ Tot
Consistency %														
Leads														
Members														
Conversion %														

Consistency Rate Scoreboard – Week 9

Monday: _____

	Budgeted Time		Growth Factors	Actual Time			Time In Minutes	
	Start	End	Budgeted Activity	Start	End	Actual Activity	Budget	Actual
1			Leads			Leads		
2			Follow-up			Follow-up		
Total								

Consistency Rate: Total Actual (A)/Budget (B)

Tuesday: _____

	Budgeted Time		Growth Factors	Actual Time			Time In Minutes	
	Start	End	Budgeted Activity	Start	End	Actual Activity	Budget	Actual
1			Leads			Leads		
2			Follow-up			Follow-up		
Total								

Consistency Rate: Total Actual (A)/Budget (B)

Wednesday: _____

	Budgeted Time		Growth Factors	Actual Time			Time In Minutes	
	Start	End	Budgeted Activity	Start	End	Actual Activity	Budget	Actual
1			Leads			Leads		
2			Follow-up			Follow-up		
Total								

Consistency Rate: Total Actual (A)/Budget (B)

Thursday: _____

	Budgeted Time		Growth Factors	Actual Time			Time In Minutes	
	Start	End	Budgeted Activity	Start	End	Actual Activity	Budget	Actual
1			Leads			Leads		
2			Follow-up			Follow-up		
Total								

Consistency Rate: Total Actual (A)/Budget (B)							
Friday: _____							
	Budgeted Time		Growth Factors	Actual Time			Time In Minutes	
	Start	End	Budgeted Activity	Start	End	Actual Activity	Budget	Actual
1	10:00am	11:00 am	Leads	10:00am	11:00 am	Leads		
2	11:00am	11:30 am	Follow-up	11:00am	11:20 am	Follow-up		
Total								
Consistency Rate: Total Actual (A)/Budget (B)							

Conversion Rate Scoreboard

Growth Factor	Monday	Tuesday	Wednesday	Thursday	Friday	Week 3
Leads (L)						
Members (M)						
Conversion Rate: M/L						

Quarterly Scoreboard

Pull from week 9 above. The average from Monday to Friday

Growth Factors	W1	W2	W3	W4	W5	W6	W7	W8	W9	W10	W11	W12	W13	Ave/Tot
Consistency %														
Leads														
Members														
Conversion %														

Consistency Rate Scoreboard – Week 10

Monday: _____							
	Budgeted Time		Growth Factors	Actual Time			Time In Minutes	
	Start	End	Budgeted Activity	Start	End	Actual Activity	Budget	Actual
1			Leads			Leads		
2			Follow-up			Follow-up		
Total								

Consistency Rate: Total Actual (A)/Budget (B)								

Tuesday: _____

	Budgeted Time		Growth Factors	Actual Time			Time In Minutes	
	Start	End	Budgeted Activity	Start	End	Actual Activity	Budget	Actual
1			Leads			Leads		
2			Follow-up			Follow-up		
Total								

Consistency Rate: Total Actual (A)/Budget (B)								

Wednesday: _____

	Budgeted Time		Growth Factors	Actual Time			Time In Minutes	
	Start	End	Budgeted Activity	Start	End	Actual Activity	Budget	Actual
1			Leads			Leads		
2			Follow-up			Follow-up		
Total								

Consistency Rate: Total Actual (A)/Budget (B)								

Thursday: _____

	Budgeted Time		Growth Factors	Actual Time			Time In Minutes	
	Start	End	Budgeted Activity	Start	End	Actual Activity	Budget	Actual
1			Leads			Leads		
2			Follow-up			Follow-up		
Total								

Consistency Rate: Total Actual (A)/Budget (B)								

Friday: _____

	Budgeted Time		Growth Factors	Actual Time			Time In Minutes	
	Start	End	Budgeted Activity	Start	End	Actual Activity	Budget	Actual
1	10:00am	11:00 am	Leads	10:00am	11:00 am	Leads		
2	11:00am	11:30 am	Follow-up	11:00am	11:20 am	Follow-up		
Total								

Consistency Rate: Total Actual (A)/Budget (B)								

Conversion Rate Scoreboard

Growth Factor	Monday	Tuesday	Wednesday	Thursday	Friday	Week 3
Leads (L)						
Members (M)						
Conversion Rate: M/L						

Quarterly Scoreboard

Pull from week 10 above. The average from Monday to Friday

Growth Factors	W1	W2	W3	W4	W5	W6	W7	W8	W9	W10	W11	W12	W13	Ave/Tot
Consistency %														
Leads														
Members														
Conversion %														

Consistency Rate Scoreboard – Week 11

Monday: _____

	Budgeted Time		Growth Factors	Actual Time			Time In Minutes	
	Start	End	Budgeted Activity	Start	End	Actual Activity	Budget	Actual
1			Leads			Leads		
2			Follow-up			Follow-up		
Total								

Consistency Rate: Total Actual (A)/Budget (B)	

Tuesday: _____

	Budgeted Time		Growth Factors	Actual Time			Time In Minutes	
	Start	End	Budgeted Activity	Start	End	Actual Activity	Budget	Actual
1			Leads			Leads		
2			Follow-up			Follow-up		
Total								

Consistency Rate: Total Actual (A)/Budget (B)	

Wednesday: _____

	Budgeted Time		Growth Factors	Actual Time			Time In Minutes	
	Start	End	Budgeted Activity	Start	End	Actual Activity	Budget	Actual
1			Leads			Leads		
2			Follow-up			Follow-up		
Total								

Consistency Rate: Total Actual (A)/Budget (B)	

Thursday: _____

	Budgeted Time		Growth Factors	Actual Time			Time In Minutes	
	Start	End	Budgeted Activity	Start	End	Actual Activity	Budget	Actual
1			Leads			Leads		
2			Follow-up			Follow-up		
Total								

Consistency Rate: Total Actual (A)/Budget (B)								
Friday: _____								
	Budgeted Time		Growth Factors	Actual Time				Time In Minutes	
	Start	End	Budgeted Activity	Start	End	Actual Activity	Budget	Actual
1	10:00am	11:00 am	Leads	10:00am	11:00 am	Leads		
2	11:00am	11:30 am	Follow-up	11:00am	11:20 am	Follow-up		
Total								
Consistency Rate: Total Actual (A)/Budget (B)								

Conversion Rate Scoreboard

Growth Factor	Monday	Tuesday	Wednesday	Thursday	Friday	Week 3
Leads (L)						
Members (M)						
Conversion Rate: M/L						

Quarterly Scoreboard

Pull from week 11 above. The average from Monday to Friday

Growth Factors	W1	W2	W3	W4	W5	W6	W7	W8	W9	W10	W11	W12	W13	Ave/Tot
Consistency %														
Leads														
Members														
Conversion %														

Consistency Rate Scoreboard – Week 12

Monday: _____								
	Budgeted Time		Growth Factors	Actual Time			Time In Minutes	
	Start	End	Budgeted Activity	Start	End	Actual Activity	Budget	Actual
1			Leads			Leads		
2			Follow-up			Follow-up		
Total								
Consistency Rate: Total Actual (A)/Budget (B)								
Tuesday: _____								
	Budgeted Time		Growth Factors	Actual Time			Time In Minutes	

	Start	End	Budgeted Activity	Start	End	Actual Activity	Budget	Actual
1			Leads			Leads		
2			Follow-up			Follow-up		
Total								

Consistency Rate: Total Actual (A)/Budget (B)

Wednesday: _____

	Budgeted Time		Growth Factors	Actual Time			Time In Minutes	
	Start	End	Budgeted Activity	Start	End	Actual Activity	Budget	Actual
1			Leads			Leads		
2			Follow-up			Follow-up		
Total								

Consistency Rate: Total Actual (A)/Budget (B)

Thursday: _____

	Budgeted Time		Growth Factors	Actual Time			Time In Minutes	
	Start	End	Budgeted Activity	Start	End	Actual Activity	Budget	Actual
1			Leads			Leads		
2			Follow-up			Follow-up		
Total								

Consistency Rate: Total Actual (A)/Budget (B)

Friday: _____

	Budgeted Time		Growth Factors	Actual Time			Time In Minutes	
	Start	End	Budgeted Activity	Start	End	Actual Activity	Budget	Actual
1	10:00am	11:00 am	Leads	10:00am	11:00 am	Leads		
2	11:00am	11:30 am	Follow-up	11:00am	11:20 am	Follow-up		
Total								

Consistency Rate: Total Actual (A)/Budget (B)

Conversion Rate Scoreboard

Growth Factor	Monday	Tuesday	Wednesday	Thursday	Friday	Week 3
Leads (L)						
Members (M)						
Conversion Rate: M/L						

Quarterly Scoreboard

Pull from week 12 above. The average from Monday to Friday

Growth Factors	W1	W2	W3	W4	W5	W6	W7	W8	W9	W10	W11	W12	W13	Ave/ Tot
Consistency %														
Leads														
Members														
Conversion %														

Consistency Rate Scoreboard – Week 13

Monday: _____

	Budgeted Time		Growth Factors	Actual Time			Time In Minutes	
	Start	End	Budgeted Activity	Start	End	Actual Activity	Budget	Actual
1			Leads			Leads		
2			Follow-up			Follow-up		
Total								

Consistency Rate: Total Actual (A)/Budget (B)

Tuesday: _____

	Budgeted Time		Growth Factors	Actual Time			Time In Minutes	
	Start	End	Budgeted Activity	Start	End	Actual Activity	Budget	Actual
1			Leads			Leads		
2			Follow-up			Follow-up		
Total								

Consistency Rate: Total Actual (A)/Budget (B)

Wednesday: _____

	Budgeted Time		Growth Factors	Actual Time			Time In Minutes	
	Start	End	Budgeted Activity	Start	End	Actual Activity	Budget	Actual
1			Leads			Leads		
2			Follow-up			Follow-up		
Total								

Consistency Rate: Total Actual (A)/Budget (B)

Thursday: _____

	Budgeted Time		Growth Factors	Actual Time			Time In Minutes	
	Start	End	Budgeted Activity	Start	End	Actual Activity	Budget	Actual
1			Leads			Leads		
2			Follow-up			Follow-up		
Total								

Consistency Rate: Total Actual (A)/Budget (B)								
Friday: _____								
	Budgeted Time		Growth Factors	Actual Time			Time In Minutes	
	Start	End	Budgeted Activity	Start	End	Actual Activity	Budget	Actual
1	10:00am	11:00 am	Leads	10:00am	11:00 am	Leads		
2	11:00am	11:30 am	Follow-up	11:00am	11:20 am	Follow-up		
Total								
Consistency Rate: Total Actual (A)/Budget (B)								

Conversion Rate Scoreboard

Growth Factor	Monday	Tuesday	Wednesday	Thursday	Friday	Week 3
Leads (L)						
Members (M)						
Conversion Rate: M/L						

Quarterly Scoreboard

Pull from week 13 above. The average from Monday to Friday

Growth Factors	W1	W2	W3	W4	W5	W6	W7	W8	W9	W10	W11	W12	W13	Ave/Tot
Consistency %														
Leads														
Members														
Conversion %														

www.ingramcontent.com/pod-product-compliance
Lightning Source LLC
Chambersburg PA
CBHW051756200326

41597CB00025B/4580